SCHOLARLY COMMUNICATION

WHAT EVERYONE NEEDS TO KNOW®

SCHOLARLY COMMUNICATION

WHAT EVERYONE NEEDS TO KNOW®

RICK ANDERSON

OXFORD
UNIVERSITY PRESS

OXFORD
UNIVERSITY PRESS

Oxford University Press is a department of the University of Oxford. It furthers the University's objective of excellence in research, scholarship, and education by publishing worldwide. Oxford is a registered trade mark of Oxford University Press in the UK and certain other countries.

"What Everyone Needs to Know" is a registered trademark of Oxford University Press.

Published in the United States of America by Oxford University Press 198 Madison Avenue, New York, NY 10016, United States of America.

© Oxford University Press 2018

Library of Congress Cataloging-in-Publication Data
Names: Anderson, Rick, 1965– author.
Title: Scholarly communication : what everyone needs to know / Rick Anderson.
Description: New York : Oxford University Press, [2018] |
Includes bibliographical references and index. |
Identifiers: LCCN 2017038743 (print) | LCCN 2017046747 (ebook) |
ISBN 9780190639464 (updf) | ISBN 9780190639471 (epub) |
ISBN 9780190639457 (pbk. : alk. paper) | ISBN 9780190639440 (cloth : alk. paper)
Subjects: LCSH: Scholarly publishing. | Academic writing. |
Authors and publishers.
Classification: LCC Z286.S37 (ebook) | LCC Z286.S37 A53 2018 (print) |
DDC 070.5—dc23
LC record available at https://lccn.loc.gov/2017038743

1 3 5 7 9 8 6 4 2

Paperback printed by Webcom, Inc., Canada
Hardback printed by Bridgeport National Bindery, Inc., United States of America

To Maggie and Tom and the next generation of scholars.

CONTENTS

3 What Does the Scholarly Communication Marketplace Look Like?   51

4 What Is Scholarly Publishing and How Does It Work?   58

6 What Is the Role of the Library? 113

13 Problems and Controversies in Scholarly Communication 224

14 The Future of Scholarly Communication 248

INTRODUCTION

Scholarly communication may seem, quite reasonably, like a narrow and specialized area of inquiry, one that most people neither need nor probably want to know very much about. So perhaps we should begin this book with what might be the most obvious question of all: *Is there anything that "everyone" really needs to know about scholarly communication?*

As we will see in Chapter 1, the term "scholarly communication" is a bit of a catch-all term that applies to a wider variety of practices and processes than one might think, and this alone suggests that scholarly communication has greater relevance to many people's lives than they know. But there is another reason to believe that there are, in fact, things about scholarly communication that everyone (or most people anyway) would benefit from knowing.

For one thing, the term "scholarly communication" refers to a culturally pervasive, complex, and widely distributed ecosystem that produces, analyzes, packages, and disseminates new scientific and scholarly knowledge. If you care about progress toward a cure for cancer, or about who wrote Shakespeare's plays, or about why particular politicians get elected in your country, or about the effects of economic policies on wages and property values, then you have (whether you know it or not) a vested interest in the scholarly communication ecosystem—its effectiveness, its efficiency, and its integrity. If you care about those things, then the ongoing debates and controversies about scholarly journal pricing, the difference between "open access" and "public access," closed versus open peer review, the proper role of copyright, and the definition of fair use all have relevance to things that you care about, and the ways those debates and controversies ultimately get resolved are going to have a concrete impact on your life.

And that is not all. If you regularly read newspapers, magazines, or websites, or if you watch news and commentary programs, you are subjected to a more or less constant discussion of important issues related to public policy, science, economics, and social trends—and within that discussion, you will be faced with a more or less constant stream of assertions about what "research tells us" or about what "the science says." To the degree that you either believe or reject such assertions, you are staking out a position on the degree to which science (not to mention the media outlets that talk about science) is a reliable source of information about reality. Why do you tend either to believe or to disbelieve such assertions? If you have an opinion one way or another as to the reliability of science and scholarship, you have (consciously or not) taken a position on the ecosystem of scholarly communication that produces scholarly and scientific analysis and disseminates it to the public.

None of this means that each of us should necessarily feel obliged to become an expert on scholarly and scientific communication, of course—but it does mean that there are issues related to scholarly communication about which it would make sense for all of us to know something. Hence this book.

What can I expect to find in this book?

Scholarly Communication: What Everyone Needs to Know is designed to be short enough not to overwhelm you with too many minutiae and too much detail, but long enough to give you a useful overview of the scholarly communication ecosystem and the full spectrum of significant issues related to it. Because it was written by a single author, it may (despite his best efforts) omit topics that another author would have considered essential; it may also (again, despite the author's best efforts) fail to account for all of the nuances of every issue and fail to present all issues with perfect accuracy and balance. Hopefully, though, it will give the general reader a useful guide to those issues and topics that pretty much everyone needs to understand at a general level in order to be an informed consumer of the documents, facts, data, and other products that the scholarly communication ecosystem creates every day, and that have an impact on our lives in ways that may not be obvious to us.

More specifically, what you will find in this book is a series of questions that the author believes might occur to a reasonably interested observer of this ecosystem— questions like "What do scholarly publishers do?" and "What is peer review?" and "How does copyright work?" The author offers answers to these questions, trying to maintain the right balance between keeping things usefully simple and honoring the reader's intelligence.

It is worth noting that there is one thing the author has tried very hard *not* to include in this book, and that is issue advocacy. One characteristic of the scholarly communication world in recent years is a growing level of controversy regarding many different issues. Open access, journal pricing, the role of libraries, the role of publishers, copyright reform, authors' rights—all of these are topics that seem to be becoming increasingly fraught, and the author has tried diligently to present the different sides of these controversies in an evenhanded and dispassionate manner. But every side in every controversy has its advocates, and it is in the nature of advocacy not to see any portrayal of a controversial issue as fair unless it favors his side. Thus, depending on their personal beliefs and perspectives, different readers may find this book's explanations of controversial topics more or less fair—and, of course, the author may not have always succeeded at presenting those topics as fairly and objectively as he has tried to.

Are there other things I won't find in this book?

The term "scholarly communication" is used advisedly in the book's title. (For an explanation of what the term means—and unfortunately, it is not as simple as one might like—see Chapter 1.) This is not a book about the publishing industry generally; you will not find any information about how literary agents work or how people come to be writers or editors for popular magazines, or about how to be a successful sports blogger or journalist, or about how publishers market their wares. The communication with which this book is concerned consists mainly of scholarly and academic writing that is disseminated through more or less formal publishing channels like scholarly and scientific journals and monographs, research reports and white papers, and conference proceedings (though we will certainly talk about scholarly blogging, preprint archiving, and other less formal publishing activities as well).

1

DEFINITIONS AND HISTORY

What is "scholarly communication" and what forms does it take?

Scholarly communication is something of an umbrella term that refers to the many different ways in which authors and creators of scholarly and scientific work share information with each other and with the rest of the world about the work they are doing. A list of the most common manifestations of scholarly communication would include the following (most of which will be discussed in more detail later in the book):

- **Articles in scholarly and scientific journals.** These are usually relatively brief reports on the results of research. These reports may reflect scientific work (reporting on laboratory research), or humanistic work (reflecting analysis of literary or artistic works), or work in the social sciences (reporting on the results of surveys, economic analysis, etc.). They are sometimes written by a single author and sometimes by several authors—in some disciplines, especially in medicine and other "hard" sciences, there may be twenty or more authors credited on a single article. The structure of research articles will vary, but especially in the science disciplines it will very often include sections reviewing the current state of the question under investigation, an explanation of the methods used to conduct the experiment, a description of the experiment itself, and discussion of the findings. As discussed below, the peer-reviewed journal article is a centrally important product of scholarly communication for most working academics in most disciplines.

- **Monographs.** The word "monograph" is not always well understood, partly because it is not always used very consistently. Generally speaking, though, the term refers to a *scholarly book* written by a *single author* dealing with a *single topic*. (The two roots of the Greek word "monograph" mean "one" and "writing.") Sometimes the phrase "scholarly monograph" is used, to make the speaker's intention clearer. Scholarly monographs are very often, though not always, published by university presses (about which more later), and they are generally written for an audience of scholars rather than for a general readership. In humanities disciplines, the monograph tends to be especially important to a scholar's academic advancement—it is often impossible to get tenure without having published a monograph with a reputable publisher.

- **Research reports.** This is something of a catch-all term that can refer to any number of very different scholarly products, but what they usually have in common is the fact that they have not been peer-reviewed or formally published in a journal. Often they are produced by think tanks, consultancies, commercial firms, or professional organizations. Sometimes these are made available to the public at no charge, and sometimes they are very expensive products sold to marketers and other professionals.

- **Preliminary versions of articles, usually shared with colleagues electronically.** These are often referred to as "preprints," though that term suggests that they are on the verge of being published, whereas in many cases what is actually being shared are preliminary drafts that have not yet even been submitted to a publisher for consideration. This kind of scholarly sharing helps authors to refine their arguments, to publicly document that they have made those arguments first (which can be tremendously important both for scientists and for scholars in the humanities and social sciences), and to reach a broader audience than would be reachable through formal publication in toll-access venues.

- **White papers.** The difference between white papers and research reports is a bit subtle, but it is important. A white paper is not usually a report of the author's research, but rather a summary of a topic designed to help a reader arrive at a conclusion. White papers may be produced by government agencies as a public service, by corporations as marketing tools, by nonprofit organizations for advocacy purposes, by consultants, and so forth. Whereas a research report should, ideally, be a relatively objective and unbiased account of a scholarly or scientific study, white papers are often designed for the purpose of leading the reader to a specific conclusion. For this reason, they may be more or less scholarly, depending on the author and the sponsor.

- **Position papers.** These are stand-alone papers that present the opinion of one or more authors on a particular issue. Position papers may be written by individuals and represent their own personal opinions, or they may be generated by an author or group of authors writing as part of an advocacy group, think tank, or other organization. Because a position paper, by definition, takes a position on the issue at hand, it is typically a tool of advocacy rather than a product of disinterested scholarship or scientific research. The authors of position papers may draw on rigorous research in the course of making their arguments—though for obvious reasons, these authors will tend to draw on research selectively rather than attempting to provide a comprehensive or strictly balanced overview of all relevant information.

- **Conference papers and presentations.** One of the most important venues for scholarly communication is the scholarly or professional conference, where scholars and scientists meet to share their findings publicly. The presentations at such conferences may take the form of papers that are read aloud, single-person presentations that are based on outlines or slides, or panel discussions (often organized as brief presentations by all of the panelists followed by a question-and-answer period with the audience). Often, but not always, these papers and presentations eventually find their way into some kind of formal publication.

- **Posters.** Not all of the presentations at academic or professional conferences are made during specific sessions in front of dedicated audiences. Very often, a conference will also feature poster presentations. These are exactly what they sound like: posters that lay out an argument or findings of a research project, usually in a highly visual way (with supporting text). The posters will typically be displayed in a large room or hallway throughout the conference, and often there will be one or more time slots dedicated to posters during the conference, during which the posters' authors will be on hand to discuss them with interested attendees. Sometimes posters are the result of program proposals that were rejected for the main program but nevertheless considered worthy of attention; sometimes they are submitted in response to a specific call for posters.

- **Conference proceedings.** While it is common for conference presentations to be formally published in journals and books, another way they may end up being published is in the proceedings of the conference. A conference proceedings is, as its name suggests, a volume that contains all (or most, but ideally all) of the papers and other presentations from a particular conference. Many annual conferences publish their proceedings every year, and libraries and readers subscribe to them as they would to a journal. Having one's paper published in a proceedings volume may carry more or less academic prestige, depending on one's discipline and on the reputation and importance of the conference itself.

- **Theses and dissertations.** The line between a student and a working scholar becomes blurred in graduate school. At the end of their programs, candidates for master's degrees generally produce theses, and doctoral candidates produce dissertations. (In some countries the terms are used vice versa.) Both are pieces of original scholarship produced under the supervision of a faculty advisor, with master's theses usually being shorter and narrower in scope, and doctoral dissertations being longer and representing more of an original contribution to the discipline. In some disciplines, particularly in the humanities and social sciences, it is common for a scholar to use her dissertation as the basis (following comprehensive revision) for her first monographic publication. After acceptance, theses and dissertations are usually made publicly available by the library of the degree-granting institution, in printed form or online or, increasingly, both.

- **Data sets.** In scholarly and scientific disciplines that rely heavily on quantitative research, the first scholarly product of the research is not a paper, but a data set. For example, if you are doing social science research using a survey instrument, your survey results are the data set initially produced by your research activities; if you are a plant biologist studying comparative growth rates among different varieties of mushroom, the data you gather from your experiments and observations represent the first product of your research. In recent years, with the development of technologies that make the sharing and repurposing of data far easier than they have ever been in the past, there has been a growing call for data themselves to be treated more like a traditional scientific output and published for public examination and reuse.

- **Multimedia works.** In some scholarly disciplines, especially in the fine arts, the final products of scholarly work may not be text-based. They may take the form of musical compositions, choreography, video, sound recordings, or some combination of these.

- **Blog postings.** There was a time, not very long ago, when the idea of a "scholarly blog" seemed laughable. Blogs, after all (the word is short for "weblog"), are basically online diaries that anyone can set up at virtually no cost and in which they can write whatever they wish. In recent years, however, blogs have evolved into something much more complex than that. The blog platform has proven to be a highly effective one for disseminating and curating not only one's personal political opinions or thoughts on the latest Gogol Bordello album, but also emerging research, professional debates on important scholarly and scientific topics, and forums for discussion between influential pundits, scientists, and scholars. (This author is himself a regular contributor to a professional blog called *The Scholarly Kitchen*, which discusses issues related to scholarly communication.) The role of the blog in academic discourse remains a controversial topic—but the fact that it is even controversial demonstrates that the blog has come up significantly in the world of scholarship.

The attentive reader may have noticed that there is no mention of classroom texts in the above. This is because although classroom texts are certainly products of scholarship, they operate in a different ecosystem and are bought and sold in a very different marketplace. Classroom texts may be produced by scholars, but they are not typical scholarly works. A scholarly article or monograph usually presumes that the reader already has a foundational understanding of the topic, whereas classroom texts assume just the opposite—in fact, they exist for the purpose of building that foundational understanding. Scholarly publications are generally written by scholars and scientists for their peers, whereas classroom texts are written for students. Scholarly monographs are expected to bring original ideas to the intellectual marketplace, whereas classroom texts are expected to synthesize and summarize existing knowledge, and so forth.

The fact that classroom texts are generally not considered part of the scholarly communication ecosystem has some interesting implications, among them the fact that academic libraries (in the United States, anyway) do not generally include textbooks in their collections. This will be discussed further in Chapter 6.

Who consumes the products of scholarly communication?

Some of the products listed above are distributed between scholars and scientists, and to the general public, more or less informally; they might be published online without any editorial intervention, or shared within a social network, or placed in archival repositories without being actively distributed at all (and might even be hidden from public view, at least for a time). Others are carefully vetted by editors and other scholars and scientists before being formally published as "versions of record."

Many, in fact most, of these scholarly and scientific products are written with colleagues and peers in mind. In fact, one of the hallmarks of scholarly communication is that the primary audience for what is being communicated is usually someone deeply knowledgeable about the topic at hand. If it were being written for people not already familiar with it, then the communication might not be considered "scholarly" at all.

Consider this book, for example. As the title of the series in which it is being published suggests, it is not primarily aimed at people who already have a deep and broad knowledge of the scholarly communication landscape; it is not, in other words, a scholarly or scientific book aimed at academics and professionals in the field. It is a general overview written for "everyone." While it might be considered an example of scholarly communication in the broadest sense, it is not the same kind of scholarly communication as what is represented by, for example, a monograph on the history of university press publishing or a peer-reviewed research study on public attitudes toward open access to scholarship.

This is not to say that scholarly communication never engages a public broader than the author's disciplinary peers and colleagues. Sometimes it does—sometimes intentionally, and sometimes unintentionally (as when a particular scholarly or scientific topic becomes urgently important as a matter of public discourse). But it is safe to say that one characteristic of scholarly communication is that it is usually aimed at a scholarly or scientific audience.

The phrase "scholarly and scientific" has already started showing up regularly here, and it is worth noting. Obviously, not all scholarly work is scientific—much of it, such as literary criticism and musical composition and language studies—is humanistic. And of course there has long been a certain amount of controversy over where the boundary lies between the "hard" sciences (like physics and geology) and the "soft" or social sciences (like economics and psychology). We are not going to negotiate those debates in this book, though they will be discussed in a bit more depth in Chapter 9. Instead, we will sidestep them in one particular sense: From this point forward, when used by itself, the word "scholarly" will stand for scholarly, academic, and research-based communication across all academic and scientific disciplines. However, there will also be points at which we will need to draw distinctions between practices, expectations, and cultures in different broad areas of science and scholarship. For the most part, we will be drawing such distinctions between the STM (scientific, technical, and medical) and HSS (humanities and social sciences) disciplines—while recognizing that not all scholarly and scientific endeavor fits neatly into one or the other of those broad categories, and that the boundaries between them remain contested.

How long have scholarly authors been communicating with each other in these ways?

It would be hard to say when the first scholarly monograph was written, but the first records of recognizable scholarly conferences suggest that they began being held in Europe in the early seventeenth century, and most historians locate the beginning of scholarly journal publishing with the establishment of *Le journal des sçavans* in Paris in 1665, which was followed shortly by the *Transactions of the Royal Society* the same year.[1] In both cases, the journals were established in order to formalize the correspondence between philosophers and scientists. Much of their communication had been by means of writing letters back and forth, but as the number of working scholars grew and the discovery and creation of scholarly knowledge began to explode, communication by correspondence became increasingly unwieldy, and the relatively recent invention of the printing press had made it practical, for the first time, to distribute copies of the same document to many people at once.

Today there are nearly 30,000 scholarly journals of various kinds in active circulation, both online and in print. The proliferation of journals over the past several centuries has been driven by the twin forces of quickly expanding scientific knowledge (which leads, inevitably, to greater and greater specialization within disciplines and a market for journals of narrower and narrower focus) and quickly advancing communication technology. Knowledge itself has expanded more gradually and steadily than communication technology has, however. In the early days of journal publishing, the technology available for communicating scholarly information was ink on paper, and journal articles were collected, edited, and bundled into issues that were sent to the journal's subscribers by mail. As late as the early 1990s, this was still the industry-standard format for scholarly communication. It wasn't until the development of the Internet in the late twentieth century, and the development of a graphical interface for it (which we call the World Wide Web), that journal publication began moving out of the print realm and into a networked digital environment—but when that change occurred, the impact on scholarly communication was seismic and nearly immediate. That impact is still being felt, and its effects inform much of the discussion elsewhere in this book.

What are the institutional contexts of scholarly communication?

Most often, when we talk about "scholars" and the ways in which they communicate, we are talking about faculty members working in the context of colleges and universities. These are scholars and scientists for whom formal communication is not only an integral part of the work they do, but also a requirement for advancement and even a condition of employment—they must publish or else they will perish. These are the ones we refer to when we talk about "tenure-track" professors: those for whom continued employment as faculty members requires them to publish new scholarship or scientific findings on a regular basis.

But not all who produce scholarship at academic institutions are on the tenure track. Some—and actually an increasing number[2]—are "adjunct" faculty members, who are employed on a year-to-year basis or may not even be full-time employees at all, but rather instructors who are paid by the course and may only be teaching one or two classes per semester. And some are not on the faculty at all, but are postdoctoral research fellows who work in labs on campus, also on a contract basis. "Postdocs" also represent a growing number of academic employees on American college campuses.[3] Both adjuncts and postdocs are likely to be actively seeking tenure-track academic appointments, and will often be involved in formal scholarly communication as a way of making themselves more attractive candidates for such jobs.

It gets more complicated still, however, because not all who produce scholarship at academic institutions are employees. Some are graduate students, who often occupy a hazy middle ground between "student" and "employee," in that they are expected to teach classes in return for a tuition waiver and perhaps also some kind of stipend. The theses and dissertations that they produce as a condition of being granted their degrees are also an important element of the scholarly communication ecosystem, and the role that those documents do and should play in that system is a matter of some controversy, which will be discussed in more detail later in this book.

But wait. It actually gets even more complicated, because we have not yet talked about the scholarly communication in which undergraduate students engage in the course of their own academic work. Undergraduates may only be scholars in embryo, but the work that they produce—especially in their upper-level courses, and especially if they are in honors programs for which they might produce a thesis of some kind toward the end of their undergraduate careers—is also being taken increasingly seriously as an example of scholarly communication.

All of the above accounts for some major parameters of the academic context of scholarly communication. But not all scholars are affiliated with academic institutions. Some operate independently of such institutions—either by choice or because they have been unable to find academic jobs—and some of these scholars publish their work formally. And it is also true that many nonacademic institutions publish scholarly and professional work of various kinds: think tanks publish reports and white papers, corporations produce research studies that may or may not be widely distributed, consulting firms publish environmental scans designed both to illuminate the landscape and to attract business, professional and scholarly societies sponsor blogs for the purpose of discussing trends and controversies in their fields, and so forth.

What all of this adds up to is a scholarly communication ecosystem rich in complexity and nuance, both inside and outside of institutional contexts. Exactly how broad and how complex this ecosystem is depends, in large part, on what one considers to be "scholarly" and on what one counts as "communication."

Wait, you just referred to scholarly communication as an "ecosystem." What do you mean by that?

We usually use the term "ecosystem" in the context of the natural ecology. However, the term also applies in terms of marketplaces. A "business ecosystem" is a "network of organizations—including suppliers, distributors, customers, competitors, government agencies and so on—involved in the delivery of a specific product or service through both competition and cooperation."[4] The world of scholarly communication is definitely an ecosystem in this sense; it operates across a highly complex landscape of organizations and individuals who contribute to it in a wide variety of ways, and who compete and cooperate with each other in an equally wide variety of ways. In Chapter 3, we will delve more deeply into the characteristics of the scholarly communication ecosystem and the different kinds of people and organizations involved in it.

What is the difference between scholarly publishing and "trade publishing"?

This is a question that might reasonably occur to someone who has overheard conversations between denizens of the scholarly communication world, or who might have a vague sense that there is something meaningfully different between, say, a book published by the University of Chicago Press and one published by HarperCollins, but cannot quite say what that difference would be.

The term "trade publication" usually refers to magazines and other professional publications aimed at people who work in specific jobs or industries. (Sometimes you will hear references to "the trades," and very often this means entertainment magazines like *Variety* and *Billboard*—magazines aimed less at fans than at entertainment professionals.)

The term "trade book" is often used in opposition to "monograph" or "scholarly monograph." (From here on, we will assume that the word "monograph" means "scholarly monograph.") A trade book is one that is published for a general readership and usually sold at a price low enough that most interested people would be able to afford it. A monograph is a scholarly book written for a scholarly audience, usually on a fairly narrow topic. Thus, a biography of Emily Dickinson is likely to be published as a trade book, whereas a close analytical reading of her poetry from 1860 to 1865 is more likely to be a monograph. (The line between trade books and scholarly monographs can be fuzzy, however.) Very often monographs are published by university presses, and in fact the term "trade press" is often used in opposition to "scholarly press" or "university press."

The term "trade paperback" is also common and has a more specific meaning: it is usually used in opposition to "mass-market paperback." A mass-market paperback is the kind once typically found in airport bookstores—small enough to fit in a coat pocket, with a glossy cover and internal pages printed on cheap and acidic newsprint-style paper. This reflects the fact that mass-market paperbacks have traditionally been treated as more or less disposable, with the expectation (not always accurate) that they will be read and thrown away rather than added to the reader's permanent collection. A trade paperback, on the other hand, is usually larger than a mass-market paperback—it will often have the same dimensions as the hardback version of the same book. Trade paperbacks are usually printed on higher-quality, acid-free paper and are designed to be appropriate for a permanent book collection. Trade paperbacks are often nonfiction and mass-market paperbacks are usually novels, but by no means are those hard-and-fast rules. And interestingly, the paperback books sold in airport bookstores are increasingly of the trade rather than mass-market variety.

How has scholarly communication changed in recent years?

As one might expect, the advent of the Internet has had a huge impact on the world of scholarly communication. In the early to mid-1990s, as the Web was maturing into a global and widely accessible locus of publishing and communication, the world of scholarly journal publishing began moving from its centuries-old print environment into the online realm. Once it began, that movement gathered momentum quickly and is now nearly complete: While many scholarly journals continue to be produced in print formats as well, the great majority of them are consumed primarily online, and it is virtually unthinkable today for a new journal to be established in a print-only format. Indeed, it is now much more common for new journals to be online only.

It is worth considering why this should be so. Why is it that print persists as an important format for scholarly book publishing but has become a marginal format for scholarly journals? One answer to this question lies in the very different structures of journals and books. A journal is essentially a series of articles, which are delivered in bundles called "issues." This bundling—which arguably makes no real sense in an online environment, where it would be quite possible simply to publish articles individually as each is finished—is an artifact of the print era, when economies of scale made it necessary to ship articles to subscribers a few times a year in bundles rather than individually. This bundling behavior tended to obscure the important fact that the basic unit of a journal is not the issue, but rather the article. And since articles are relatively small and compact units of scholarship, they are easy to consume in online formats: They can usually be read online without difficulty, or downloaded and printed for offline reading later.

Obviously, the same is not true of scholarly books, which tend to be long, linear, and detailed developments of specific ideas and arguments. Although e-book readers continue to grow in popularity, they are used mostly for casual and popular reading. While a large and growing number of people are showing themselves willing to read a crime novel on an e-book reader, it is not yet clear that online formats provide the best platform for reading a 400-page exposition on the late correspondence of Emily Dickinson. For these and other reasons, journal publishing made the online shift quickly, but scholarly books took quite a bit longer to make that jump, and in fact e-books are still not the default manifestation of scholarly books today—although almost all scholarly monographs are now published as both e-books and print books, and a growing proportion of sales of scholarly books (both to libraries and to individuals) is in digital formats.

The nearly wholesale migration of scholarly communication from print to online has been interesting for a variety of reasons. One of the interesting things about that migration is that it has been simultaneously hugely disruptive and not disruptive at all. What does that mean? First of all, it would be difficult to overstate the enormous difference made to scholarly communication by the migration of its documentary manifestations (articles, white papers, books, etc.) out of the physical and into the online realm. Printed books and journal issues offer a convenient and pleasurable reading experience and a relatively stable archival medium; however, ink on paper is a terrible mechanism for distributing information to lots of people (think about the time and cost involved in making printed books available to, say, 500,000 readers) and it is also a very poor format for those who are doing research, as opposed to simply reading. After all, the only way to search the full text of a printed document is to read the whole thing, and it is very common that scholars and students need to find discrete pieces of information inside very long documents. To suggest that a scholar or scientist should read every page of every document relevant to her research would be absurd. (Some printed books have indexes, of course, but even the best index provides only a crude and schematic guide to the full content of a book.) As scholarly and scientific documents have moved from the print to the online realm, they have become radically easier to find and to interrogate, and they have become available to a radically larger number of people. The importance and impact of this shift cannot be overstated.

However, some things about scholarly communication have changed very little in the wake of the Internet revolution. Although the rise of the Internet and its gradual establishment as the default matrix for all kinds of communication have made possible many kinds of new publishing tools and initiatives (blogs, e-mail listservs, chat boards, preprint archives, repositories, etc.), those developments have done little to change some of the most fundamental aspects of scholarly communication. Today, just as in 1979, if you are a humanist scholar, you are almost certainly going to have to publish a monograph with a university press in order to get tenure. Today, just as in 1979, the peer-reviewed journal article remains the "coin of the realm" for tenure and promotion in the physical and biological sciences—and those articles are still usually bundled together into virtual journal issues, despite the fact that such bundling serves no real purpose and makes no obvious sense in an online context. Editors, authors, and peer reviewers are now able to communicate with each other much more quickly and easily than they could back when they had to do so by mail or by phone, but all of them still do more or less the same things that they did in 1950—they just do them (for the most part) somewhat more quickly and efficiently, using more effective tools. Some in the worlds of academia and applied research have called for a more radical rethinking of some of these persistent practices, but so far with little effect. That may not remain so forever.

Another thing that changed very little during the initial stages of the Internet revolution was the fact that access to scholarly publications was available only to those who could (or were willing to) pay for it. This arrangement was less controversial when information was bound up in physical documents that were expensive to print and distribute. It has become increasingly more controversial as the Internet has made it possible to distribute functionally unlimited copies of documents at effectively zero marginal cost. The open access (OA) movement arose, in part, in response to this new reality; that movement is discussed in more detail in Chapter 12.

In short, over the past few decades the course of change and development in scholarly communication has been a strangely diverse one, as some foundational aspects of that ecosystem have experienced deep and even existential change while other aspects have remained substantially unaffected. However, the Internet revolution has created changes elsewhere—largely outside what we usually think of as the realm of scholarly communication—that are likely to continue to have an impact within that realm and that may yet create radical and disruptive change within it. Some of these possible developments will be discussed later in this book.

2

WHO ARE THE SCHOLARS AND WHY DO THEY COMMUNICATE?

Who contributes to the scholarly communication ecosystem?

First of all, it is important to note that scholarly communication does, in fact, take place within an ecosystem, a complex one that includes many different players. Some of the most important of these are as follows.

Scholars and scientists do the work about which they are communicating. Historians, research chemists, literature professors, geneticists, sociologists, linguists, clinical oncologists—all of these contribute the fruits of their scholarly and scientific work to the ecosystem of scholarly communication, and they do so in a variety of ways.

Institutions employ those scholars and scientists. Most of the scholars and scientists who contribute to the scholarly communication ecosystem are paid a salary as employees of sponsoring institutions like colleges, universities, research foundations, and hospitals. The intellectual output that they produce in their various capacities as employees of those institutions is the lifeblood of the scholarly communication ecosystem, which means that the salaries they are paid by those institutions represent a very significant input into the ecosystem.

Funding agents make decisions about what scholarly and scientific work to support (and about the conditions and rules under which the support will be provided). While scholars and scientists are usually paid a salary by their host institutions, in some fields of study those salaries are not sufficient to cover the costs of doing applied research. In these fields, researchers are expected to bring in grant funding from governmental or private funding bodies. Doing so not only supports their research directly but also contributes to the support of their host institutions— because research grants usually include money to cover overhead costs such as lab upkeep and wages for research assistants. However, typical levels of grant funding will vary greatly from discipline to discipline: A researcher working in an advanced field of applied study such as high-energy physics might bring in multiple millions of grant dollars in a typical year, whereas a scholar of American literature might work largely without grant funding. The central importance of grant funding in certain disciplines means that the foundations and agencies that provide research grants have a significant influence over the shape of scientific discourse in those disciplines, and little if any influence in others.

Government agencies make decisions about what can and cannot be done with scholarly products arising from research supported with public funding. While private funding organizations can set their own rules about the disposition of publications produced with the funding they provide, government agencies have less independence and are often subject to requirements set by overarching policy. One example of this dynamic can be seen in the White House Office of Science and Technology memorandum on "Increasing Access to the Results of Federally-funded Research."[1] This communication directs all U.S. agencies that provide more than $100 million annually in research funding to develop and submit a plan showing how they will "ensure that the public can read, download, and analyze in digital form final peer-reviewed manuscripts or final published documents within a timeframe that is appropriate for each type of research conducted or sponsored by the agency."

Interest groups and lobbyists work to influence government and funder policies. The shape of both public and private funding policies is influenced significantly by the lobbying and advocacy activities of organizations dedicated to changing (or preserving) particular characteristics of the scholarly communication ecosystem. Organizations like the Scholarly Publishing and Academic Resources Coalition (SPARC) and the Center for Open Data Enterprise advocate for greater freedom of access to scholarly publications and data; organizations like the Association of American Publishers and the Copyright Alliance tend to focus their efforts on protecting the interests of copyright holders and traditional publishers.

Publishers turn raw manuscripts into formal publications, market them, curate their content, and sell them to individuals and libraries. For reasons that will be discussed in subsequent chapters, publishers have a tremendous influence over the shape and content of scholarly communication. They are the organizations that select, prepare, and distribute the books and articles that are generally considered the "coin of the realm" of scholarly and scientific discourse, and very prestigious publishers who attract lots of authors thereby wield a particularly outsized influence over that discourse. (As we shall see, there is a wide variety of opinion within the scholarly community about whether and to what degree this is a healthy state of affairs.) However, it is also worth noting that with the emergence of the Internet as the default locus of publication and communication, other channels of scholarly communication have emerged as well, such as blogs, pre-print archives, and institutional repositories. Some of these operate symbiotically with traditional, formal publication channels, and some directly compete with them.

Editors and peer reviewers (some of whom are employed by publishers, but many of whom are faculty members at universities and colleges) act as mediators between scholarly and scientific authors and publishers. Editors receive submissions from authors and, in some cases, decide unilaterally which submissions will be accepted and which ones will be rejected; in other cases, they distribute the submissions to peer reviewers for an additional layer of review consideration before making a final decision. (See Chapter 4 for more detailed discussion of this practice.) Once an article or book is accepted for publication, the editor works with the author to refine both its content and its presentation, a process that can take quite some time—in extreme cases, even years.

Scholarly and scientific societies provide networking to scholarly authors, hold conferences, and, very often, act as publishers themselves. (In the United Kingdom, these are typically referred to as "learned societies," whereas in the United States they are more commonly called "scholarly," "scientific," or "professional" societies.) Societies are tremendously important to scholars and scientists. When thinking about scholarly behavior, especially when it comes to publication and other forms of scholarly communication, it is essential to remember that for many if not most working scholars, their deepest and primary allegiance is to their discipline rather than to the particular institution that employs them.[2] Institutional affiliation is contingent, whereas disciplinary affiliation is usually permanent. In other words, a biologist may be a member of the faculty at the University of Chicago one year and at the University of North Carolina a year later—but she will always be a biologist. For this reason, organizations like the American Institute of Biological Sciences or the Royal Society of Biology are likely to command a deeper loyalty than either of those universities, and this fact will have implications for the choices she makes about where and how to publish.

Libraries buy books and journals and make them available to students and faculty. The roles played by academic libraries in scholarly communication—of which there are more than one might think—are discussed in depth in Chapter 6. Here it is worth noting that one of the fundamental roles played by the library is that of broker: Working scholars and scientists typically need access to far more information resources than they could possibly afford to purchase (and house and care for) themselves, so by building and funding libraries their institutional communities create centralized stores of research materials that all of their affiliated students, scholars, and scientists may use. The changing nature of the scholarly communication ecosystem and drastic shifts in research behavior on the part of both students and scholars have had serious implications for library practice, and these too will be discussed later in the book.

Obviously, all of these players contribute to the system in different ways, and their various contributions interlock with each other and are interdependent in varying degrees. For example, publishers rely on authors to supply them with content, and they compete with each other to attract the best authors. Authors trade publication rights (often including a complete transfer of copyright) to publishers in exchange for the editing, review, and certification services publishers provide, and they compete with each other for placement in the most highly regarded journals or (in the case of books) publication with the most prestigious publishers. Students and faculty rely on their libraries to pay for subscriptions to journals and books that they cannot afford to buy for themselves, and to house and care for those documents (or to broker reliable online access to them). Libraries try to figure out how to balance the needs of their patrons both as consumers and as creators of scholarly information, all the while wrestling with (often stagnant) budgets in an environment of (always rising) prices. Government and funding agencies that underwrite research look for ways to maximize the positive societal impact of that research, and accordingly set rules that have impacts on authors, publishers, and the general public. Interest groups and lobbyists try to convince those agencies that particular rules will maximize public benefit more effectively than others. And so forth.

This ecosystem has always been complex, but it became markedly more so with the advent of the World Wide Web in the early to mid-1990s. The Web made it possible, for the first time, to make documents easily accessible to billions of people simultaneously, and to distribute copies of those documents en masse at virtually no marginal added cost per copy. Almost immediately, journal publication began moving into the online realm—though it has taken some time for journal publishing to leave print entirely behind, and journals still have not done so entirely. Although a diminishing percentage of journals continue to be distributed both in print and online, the prospects for a 100% online journal publishing environment remain distant. As nearly ubiquitous as the Internet is, online access remains spotty in developing regions of the world, and publishers face declining but still ongoing demand for access to journal content in print. This means that they must continue dealing with multiple production workflows, which adds complexity and cost to an already difficult and expensive process.

The persistence of dual-format publishing creates complexity and expense for libraries as well. No longer is the library simply a building filled with physical documents;

it is now also a broker of access to online documents, and the online collections to which the typical academic library provides access are many times larger than the physical collection. This has required librarians to take on many new roles and acquire many new skills, including license negotiation, troubleshooting authentication systems, and database administration. At the same time, the physical collection continues both to take up space and to demand care even as its usage levels decline.

For the scholars and researchers themselves, the new scholarly communication ecosystem offers both expanded opportunities and new complications and even dangers. The relatively low startup cost of online publishing has led to an explosion in new journals, which provides more publishing opportunities but has also made it more difficult to discriminate between high- and low-quality outlets (and even outright publishing scams, which have proliferated in recent years and are discussed further in Chapter 13). Furthermore, online access makes it possible to track more accurately when an article is read or cited, which means that it is (in theory, anyway) possible to measure the real-world impact of an article in ways heretofore unimagined. This has led to new tools that compete with each other for acceptance, and to new institutional and governmental policies that are not always received with joy by everyone in the system—least of all authors. And while online publishing makes dissemination much cheaper and easier, it does little to reduce the costs of marketing, while creating new roles that publishers are expected to take on, such as serving as a permanent archive of content.

What is the difference between a college and a university?

The usage of these two terms (and the degree to which they are used interchangeably in casual conversation) varies somewhat from country to country. In the United States, the phrase "going to college" is commonly used in a generic way to indicate the advancement from secondary to tertiary education—thus, if one were to ask an acquaintance "Where did you go to college?" the answer might be "At the University of Michigan," and no one would find that answer confusing. However, there is a real and meaningful distinction between colleges and universities—or, to be more accurate, there are multiple meaningful distinctions between those terms, distinctions that vary by context and that truly can be confusing.

One common line of demarcation between colleges and universities is by institution type. In the United States, a university is invariably at least a four-year institution that grants bachelor's degrees. Universities also typically host postgraduate programs that grant master's and doctoral degrees. By contrast, in this context a college is usually a two- or four-year institution. Community colleges usually offer open admission (meaning that anyone with a high school diploma is eligible to matriculate) and offer two-year courses of study and award associate's degrees. Community colleges also tend to serve an important function in providing both professional certification programs and remediation for those students who require additional preparation before enrolling at a university or four-year college. Four-year colleges often focus on the liberal arts rather than the applied sciences, and emphasize classroom instruction rather than research.

What are Carnegie classifications and what do they mean?

The Carnegie Classification of Institutions of Higher Education is a system created in 1973 by the Carnegie Foundation for the Advancement of Teaching. (In 2014, the Foundation transferred responsibility for the system to Indiana University Bloomington's Center for

Postsecondary Research.[3]) Its purpose is to place institutions into broad categories that reflect their missions, their relative focus with regard to teaching or research, the years of instruction they offer, and so forth.[4] The seven basic Carnegie classifications are as follows:

Tribal Colleges: These represent a mix of colleges and universities, all belonging to the American Indian Higher Education Consortium.

Special Focus Institutions: These represent a mix of two- and four-year institutions, all of which feature a high degree of disciplinary specialization. They include law schools, medical schools, colleges of art and design, technical schools, and other highly specialized institutions, all of which generally have a focus on professional preparation and certification rather than a broader liberal arts education.

Associate's Colleges: Often referred to as community colleges, these are distinguished by the fact that the degree they offer is a two-year associate's degree. They are further subcategorized into those that focus on traditional liberal education, those that focus on technical education, and those that offer various mixtures of the two.

Baccalaureate/Associate's Colleges: These schools offer at least one bachelor's degree program; they are further subdivided into those that mix bachelor's and associate's degree programs somewhat evenly and those that focus primarily on associate's programs.

Baccalaureate Colleges: This category includes institutions in which at least 50% of the degrees awarded are bachelor's degrees or higher; fewer than fifty master's degrees or twenty doctoral degrees are awarded annually. Most of what are commonly referred to as liberal arts colleges fit into this category.

Master's Colleges and Universities: A college or university that awards more than fifty master's degrees but fewer than twenty doctoral degrees annually is given this designation. These are subdivided into categories M3, M2, and M1 (representing smaller, medium-sized, and larger programs).

Doctoral Universities: These universities award twenty or more doctoral degrees annually. Like the Master's Colleges and Universities, institutions in this category are subdivided by research activity: R3 (moderate), R2 (higher), and R1 (highest). "Research activity" is measured according to a number of criteria, including research and development expenditures in various science fields, size of research (as opposed to teaching) staff, and doctoral degree conferrals across all disciplines.[5]

As one might expect, the Carnegie category into which a particular institution falls will correlate to a real degree with the ways in which scholars and scientists at that institution interact with the scholarly communication ecosystem. Faculty at doctoral universities are more likely to be heavily involved in producing publishable scholarship, for example, while those at an associate's college will tend to function more as consumers than as producers of original scholarly work.

How are universities organized?

Another important sense in which we distinguish between colleges and universities is one that applies within the organizational structure of the university itself. In the traditional English model, a university is actually a constellation of colleges, each of which operates with a greater or lesser degree of independence from the others (and from the university organization as a whole). At the more extreme end of this model lie Oxford and Cambridge Universities in England; in each case, the component colleges have particular curricular emphases, but these emphases are not reflected in the names of the colleges. The American model tends to retain the basic structure of colleges-within-a-university, but the colleges are usually much less structurally independent and tend to be identified by discipline: the College of Humanities, the College of Law, and so forth. In American universities it is also quite common for colleges to have "schools" within them; thus, a university might have a College of Fine Arts within which exists a School of Music, and a College of Earth Sciences within which there is a School of Mines. More typically, however, a college is made up of departments, and what distinguishes a "school" from a "department" may be somewhat unclear and may vary from institution to institution.

To make things even more ambiguous, there are institutions of higher education that are neither colleges nor universities. The variety of such institutions is quite broad, but one important example is represented by private research institutes like the Massachusetts Institute of Technology and the California Institute of Technology. (These should not be confused with the Georgia Institute of Technology, generally known as Georgia Tech, which actually is a public university.)

Another important variety of higher-education institution is represented by the for-profit colleges, universities, and institutes—some accredited and some not—that provide both traditional degree programs and professional certification, usually online (though also sometimes on "campuses" located in storefronts and office buildings). These institutions have come under increasing scrutiny in recent years. Some have been accused of using overly aggressive recruitment tactics and making unrealistic promises about the job prospects that graduates can expect to have, and some charge what seem to be exorbitant tuition rates. Several of the largest for-profit higher-education institutions in the United States have lost accreditation and have shut down recently under this pressure. Nevertheless, the for-profit sector remains an important facet of the system of higher education, and at its best it serves an important function within that system. This sector is not, however, a significant player in the production and publication of scholarly documents—for-profit colleges do not have university presses and are much less likely to require their faculty to publish original works of scholarship.

What exactly is tenure, and why do scholars and scientists want it?

No conversation about scholarly communication goes on for very long before the concept of "tenure and promotion" comes up. This is because many if not most academic authors spend the first part of their careers either trying to get onto the tenure track, or (having gotten there) trying to secure tenure so that they can remain employed. Especially during this period of their careers, choices they make regarding scholarly communication will be substantially shaped by that goal.

So what is tenure? It is, essentially, a state of permanent employment. When a young scholar or scientist is hired into a tenure-track position (usually at the rank of assistant professor), the expectation is that he will prove himself as a scholar, scientist, and/or instructor for anywhere from five to seven years, at the end of which he will either be granted tenure and kept as a member of the faculty indefinitely, or not granted tenure and his contract terminated. Usually, one is granted tenure simultaneously with promotion to the rank of associate professor. Thus, the tenure-track system is a classic example of an "up or out" arrangement—one is either promoted at the end of an appointed period of time, or one is let go.

All of this would be sufficient to explain why scholars and scientists want tenure. The reason this issue is relevant to a discussion of scholarly communication is that publishing one's scholarly or scientific work in reputable venues is, in most disciplines, essential to securing tenure. Publishing in such venues is how an assistant professor demonstrates to his academic colleagues that his work has been deemed worthy by colleagues elsewhere in the discipline, and a strong publication record is one of the first things that a faculty committee will look for when considering that professor's bid for tenure.

But there is another very important reason that tenure is important to faculty, and it has to do with academic freedom. This point will be discussed more fully later in this chapter.

It is important to note that many academic faculty members are not on the tenure track, but rather are adjunct or temporary employees. Adjuncts are typically employed for one or two years at a time, and are often paid according to the number of classes they teach rather than given a flat salary. In recent years, the proportion of adjuncts to tenure-track faculty has rapidly grown, partly because adjuncts can be paid much less and partly because the number of newly minted PhDs has grown enormously relative to the number of tenure-track positions available. Adjuncts are, for obvious reasons, very often eager to get onto the tenure track, and will try to establish a strong record of scholarly publication to help themselves do so.

It is also important to note that—despite the rhetoric one might encounter in the popular press about "professors with their cushy permanent jobs from which they cannot be fired"—when it comes to tenure, "permanent employment" does not mean "guaranteed permanent employment no matter what." Getting tenure does not mean that you cannot be fired for cause, and it does not even mean that you cannot be laid off. It means that the college or university has decided to retain you on an ongoing basis; however, if you are a faculty member, your performance will still be subject to regular review and evaluation, and if you fail to do your job you can be fired. Faculty can also be laid off in the event that their institutions come under severe financial pressure. All of that said, the popular press is not usually wrong to point out that firing tenured faculty is difficult—as, indeed, it is supposed to be. This leads to our next question.

Granted that academics want tenure, why do academic institutions want to award it? What is in it for the institution?

The most commonly invoked justification for a tenure system is that it preserves academic freedom—the freedom to say, write, and teach according to one's beliefs and one's best professional judgment. Although tenured faculty may be fired for cause (for consistently failing to show up to teach their classes, say, or for committing acts of academic malfeasance), they usually may not be fired for teaching things that the dean or the university president disagrees with, or for writing controversial books, or for adopting particular political viewpoints. Furthermore, it is generally taken as an article of faith in academic institutions that the faculty determine the content of all teaching—courses are not designed nor is their content determined by the college or university administration. Faculty members may be told which classes they will teach and when those classes will be held, but they are free to decide for themselves both what information the courses will contain and the manner in which the courses will be taught.

This arrangement benefits not only the faculty but also the institution, because it enhances the institution's reputation for academic excellence and makes it easier to attract top-quality academic talent. Although administrators will often complain about the difficulty of dealing with tenured faculty, it is rare (though not unheard of) for them to try to dismantle the tenure system in their institutions.

What all of this means is that it is, indeed, difficult to fire tenured faculty members. Such firings happen relatively rarely, and when they do, it is invariably after a long, convoluted, and politically difficult process that is overseen by at least one (and often more) committees of the faculty as well as institutional administrators. In addition to determining the content of the campus curriculum, it is the faculty's job to say who will and will not join the ranks of faculty and who will be permitted to stay, and such decisions are not made lightly. (At most academic institutions, the campus president or chancellor will ratify the faculty's tenure decisions and often a board of regents also must approve those decisions—but in the great majority of cases, these ratifications are a rubber-stamp process. The real decision is made by the faculty.)

What does scholarly communication look like?

We have already made reference to many of the typical documents and other outputs that populate the scholarly communication ecosystem, but in this section we will examine their characteristics and their variety a bit more closely.

In the STM disciplines, one of the most common and basic units of scholarly communication is the peer-reviewed journal article. Peer review is an exceptionally important concept in scholarly communication. Simply put, peer review is a system under which an author's submitted manuscript is given to one or more of the author's professional peers for vetting prior to any final editorial decision. The thinking behind this approach is that while journal editors are usually knowledgeable about the discipline generally (and about their own disciplinary subfields in particular), they cannot possibly know enough about every area of their discipline to be able to fully evaluate every paper submitted. And if the journal is a popular one that publishes only a small percentage of submitted articles, the challenges of scale make it necessary to farm out some of the early stage evaluation of those submissions. Thus, peer reviewers provide a sort of rough-cut editorial service, letting editors know which articles are worth serious editorial attention and which are not. Very often peer review is "blind" (which is to say that the author does not know who is reviewing her submission) and sometimes it is "double blind" (which means that the reviewer also does not know who the author is). As mentioned above, the mechanisms of peer review will be discussed in a bit more detail in Chapter 4 of this book.

In the humanities, articles are also important. However, for most tenure-seeking faculty members, it is essential to publish a monograph, usually with a university press. Publishing a scholarly monograph is not sufficient to secure tenure, but in many humanistic (and some social science) fields it would be very difficult to secure tenure without doing so.

Not all important scholarly communication is published in journals or books, however—in fact, not all of it is formally published at all. As the Web has matured, it has begun offering more varied and more reliable outlets for the communication of scholarly information, both between scholars and between scholars and the general public. One of the most important and well-known venues for informal scholarly communication is a preprint repository called arXiv (pronounced "archive," because what looks like a capital letter X in the middle of the word is really the Greek letter *chi*). Preprint repositories will be discussed again in Chapter 4, but the particular history of arXiv is worth noting here. Established in 1991 by Paul Ginsparg at Los Alamos National Laboratory, arXiv is something of an online swap meet for authors of research articles in the fields of physics, mathematics, computer science, nonlinear sciences, quantitative biology, and statistics.[6] Here authors can share preliminary versions of their research articles and get input from their colleagues, and the papers they share are freely available to the general public as well. Submissions are subjected to a light version of peer review (in order to weed out content not appropriate for the venue) but are not otherwise edited by arXiv staff or moderators. Many of the preliminary papers deposited in arXiv are later published formally, in their final versions of record, in journals. In 2011 arXiv moved from Los Alamos to the library at Cornell University, and in recent years a number of similarly configured preprint servers have arisen to serve other science fields, including bioRXiv, PsyArXiv, SocArXiv, and engrXiv.

The Web has also given rise to the blog, which has had a significant impact on scholarly communication over the past decade. Originally known as "weblogs," blogs are essentially online diaries; many companies offer free blogging accounts (the most popular platforms include WordPress and Blogspot) that allow users to sign up and write whatever they wish in a preformatted online space, and allow readers to make comments as well. Over time, however, blogs have become an important locus of serious scholarly and scientific discourse. The term "scholarly blog" no longer gives rise to derision or hilarity, and quite a few professional and learned societies maintain blogs in which they discuss important issues. One of the significant functions that blogs have come to serve is as a debate platform—papers that are published formally in journals are regularly discussed, dissected, and critiqued on relevant blogs. Scientists and scholars with a particular gift for punditry have even managed to build large followings of readers for their personal blogs, which in turn lead readers to their formal publications. Sometimes journals will establish companion blogs, and there are even formally published online journals that are themselves built on blogging platforms.

The listserv is another form of scholarly communication that has been made possible by the rise of the Internet and that has had significant impacts on scholars' ability to communicate with each other. A listserv is basically an e-mail discussion group; subscribe to it and you immediately become party to an ongoing conversation about developments in your discipline, notable controversies, upcoming events, and so forth. Some scholarly and professional listservs are subdued and generate only a few messages per month; others are more freewheeling and rancorous and may generate scores (or even hundreds) of messages per day. Listservs are usually archived online, and while their content is never considered authoritative or even formal, they can contribute in very important ways to the development of the thinking in a discipline.

Scholars also communicate with each other in person, both informally on a one-on-one basis and more formally in the context of professional conferences where papers and research results are shared through presentations. Often the papers presented at conferences are later published formally—sometimes in journals, and sometimes in conference proceedings volumes that document the information presented in the conference itself. And, of course, scholars communicate with each other from a distance by means of mail, e-mail, and phone, exchanging ideas and sharing preliminary findings and copies of their published work.

You mentioned the "version of record" just now—what does that mean?

With the emergence of the Internet as the primary locus of scholarly communication, version control has become a major problem in scholarly communication. This problem is the flipside to one of the major benefits of Internet-based communication: the ease and speed with which documents can be duplicated and the copies distributed. Since science and scholarship depend for their vitality on more or less constant communication between scientists and scholars, the Internet has added greatly to the vibrancy of scholarly communication and the speed at which scholarly conversations may be conducted—and thus has also contributed to a constantly growing chaotic mass of document versions.

To get a sense of the scope of this problem, suppose that you are a social scientist working in the field of social psychology. You have conducted a major study of depression in the populations of three large, geographically diverse cities and have found interesting similarities and differences in the dynamics within and between those populations. Now suppose that you write a preliminary report of those findings and distribute it by e-mail to a handful of trusted colleagues or post it in a preprint repository (like SocArXiv), soliciting input from your peers on its strengths and weaknesses. Based on their input, you adjust your presentation and tighten up your arguments, and you submit the resulting revised version to a peer-reviewed journal for publication. The editor sends your submission to a couple of peer reviewers, who respond with suggestions of their own. Those suggestions are sent back to you with a request that you revise the article again, which you do. You then submit a new version to the editor. That version (often referred to as the "author's accepted manuscript") is accepted for publication. A few months later you receive a typeset and fully formatted version of the article with a request that you review it for errors prior to publication; you find a few errors (including a couple of poorly phrased sentences and some assertions that need to be softened just a bit) and return the corrected proof. Finally, the article is published in a version that reflects those last corrections.

Over the course of the process described above—which is a pretty typical one for most scholarly and scientific authors—you will have created no fewer than five versions of your article: the preliminary report you shared with colleagues; the initial version originally submitted for publication; the revision taking into account suggestions from the reviewers; the typeset and formatted version reflected in the uncorrected proof; and the final version reflecting your proof corrections. Some of those versions (such as the uncorrected proof) are unlikely ever to be seen again by you or anyone else. Other versions, however, may find their way online by various means, either in whole or in part: One of your colleagues might quote a paragraph from your preliminary report in a listserv posting; you might deposit the approved manuscript version in your local institutional repository; the final, published version will of course be published online and may become freely available to the public, either immediately or after an embargo period; and so forth. Furthermore, you may at some point create a PowerPoint-based description of your article's methodology and findings and present it at a conference using the same title for your presentation as the one under which your article was published—and *voilà*, version number six.

With multiple versions of your article essentially floating around in cyberspace, the question of which version is the authoritative one—the one that reflects all of the tweaks and corrections that you became convinced were necessary over the long course of your article's journey to final publication—becomes crucial. When your colleague quoted a paragraph from your preliminary report, was it a paragraph that you subsequently changed in some important way before the final article was published? Did you make material changes to your text at some point between the submission of your accepted manuscript and the submission of your corrected proof? (If you are an author with long publishing experience, the answer to that question is almost certainly yes—this author once caught a small typographical error in an uncorrected proof that, had it not been fixed, would have reversed the argument he was trying to make in that paragraph.)

The official, authoritative version of an article is referred to as the "version of record." Unsurprisingly, it is almost always the final, fully formatted, formally published version that appears in the journal. For equally obvious reasons, it is always the one that should be cited by other scholars. This does not mean that it is the only useful version; depending on one's purposes in consulting it, the author's accepted manuscript or some other preprint version may be perfectly acceptable. But in the scholarly communication ecosystem, it is the version of record that is generally regarded as the one that should be regarded as final and authoritative.

Why do scholars go to the effort of communicating in these ways?

Informal scholarly communication—blog posts, phone calls with colleagues, sending a draft article to a friend, hallway conversation at conferences—can be quite quick and easy, and is often an effective way simply to share information. Formal scholarly communication, whether in the form of monographs or research articles or other kinds of published products, is invariably both labor-intensive and time-consuming. Why do scholars do it?

There is more than one reason, of course. For scholars who are tenure-track faculty members, formal publication is usually a job requirement: If you do not publish that book with a university press or publish a certain number of articles in well-regarded peer-reviewed journals, you will not get tenure and will be out of work. For scholars in this situation, formal publication is a means of certification: It demonstrates that one's work is recognized by one's peers in the profession as being high-quality and high-relevance scholarship.

For scholars who are not on the tenure track but wish to be, formal publication serves the purpose of making them more attractive candidates for appointment. As the number of adjunct instructors and postdoctoral fellows on college campuses continues to grow, this function may increase in importance. In many academic fields, the market for tenure-track positions is extremely tough, and those who want jobs in academia will often settle for temporary appointments as instructors or adjunct professors, or will take postdoctoral research fellowships as a means of getting their foot in the door. For early career academics in this kind of situation, formal publication is more than just a means of sharing the content of their research with peers and colleagues—it is also a way of demonstrating their intellectual seriousness and scholarly accomplishment to those who will be considering them in the future as job candidates. The importance of this aspect of scholarly communication—its role as a self-branding and certification process for aspiring and tenure-track academics—cannot be overstated.

Of course, scholars also want their work to be read, and to have an impact in their fields and beyond. Prior to the advent of the World Wide Web, the most effective and efficient way to distribute one's work to an interested audience was to place it in the most well-regarded publishing venues—but, with a handful of highly read exceptions, even the most highly regarded academic journals had only a relatively few readers. Today, simply making one's work findable and accessible to the broadest possible audience is a much simpler matter: Put it online and billions of people will immediately be able to read it (though making it easily findable requires a bit more work than that). This issue, and how scholars decide where to place their work, will be discussed further in Chapter 4.

Why is formal scholarly communication expensive and labor-intensive?

One might reasonably ask why it is that, in the age of the Internet—with its free blogging accounts, instantaneous e-mail delivery, listservs, and preprint repositories—formal scholarly communication is still a slow and laborious (and therefore expensive) proposition. There are at least two answers to this question, one of them more satisfactory and one of them less so.

The less satisfactory answer is that scholarly publishing is a field that is slow to change—almost as slow as academia itself. While in recent years there have been notable experiments in fairly radical reworkings of such traditional publishing forms as the scholarly journal and the monograph (some of which will be discussed in detail elsewhere in this book), the predominant structures within which *formal* scholarly communication takes place still look very much the way they did fifty years ago: journals that are edited and peer-reviewed in essentially the way they always were and that are published in monthly, quarterly, or semiannual issues, and monographs that, even when available as e-books, still look and feel quite a bit like printed monographs. To say that these formats and structures are old-fashioned is not necessarily to say that they are outmoded—they preserve aspects of scholarly publishing that are inarguably valuable—but there is no denying that they are labor-intensive and time-consuming. It is a widely held view in the world of academia and publishing that they have not evolved as quickly or fully as they should.

The more satisfactory answer is that when it comes to accomplishing the tasks that most consider essential to the integrity and quality of scholarly products, there are not very many shortcuts available. For example, although the peer-review process is not without its detractors, and there have been attempts to come up with alternatives to it, peer review is still generally regarded as the gold standard of scholarly certification for journal articles (and, to some degree, scholarly monographs as well). When one considers the simple problem of scale, it becomes clear why this should be so: No journal can employ all of the editors that would be necessary to thoroughly vet every article submission—there are, in most cases, simply too many, and they come in too wide a variety of subspecialties. Furthermore, the number of submissions is generally growing and subspecialties continue to proliferate. The solution to this scale problem is delegation or outsourcing: External peer reviewers volunteer their time and expertise in reviewing article submissions thoroughly, passing their recommendations back to the editor. Very rarely are they paid directly for this work; they are mainly academics who perform these review duties during work or personal time on a voluntary basis, understanding that they are both contributing to the scholarly enterprise as a whole and also building up karma for when an article of their own needs to be reviewed by another volunteer somewhere else.

This system is fraught with problems, of course. For one thing, many more articles must be reviewed than will ultimately be published, meaning that a tremendous amount of reviewers' work results not in an article or book being made available, but in preventing its availability. Managing the peer-review process itself—keeping track of which articles have gone out for review and to whom, following up when reviewers are slow to respond (or never respond at all, even after accepting the assignment), acting on reviewers' suggestions (which often then leads to a second round of reviewing after revisions have been made), dealing with authors who disagree with proposed revisions—is an exceptionally time-consuming process that can be emotionally draining as well. Most editors are themselves academics with full-time jobs, and many are not paid for their editorial services; they provide them in much the same spirit that volunteer peer reviewers do, though they also get the benefit of a nice entry on their professional curriculum vitae, one that will help them get tenure or advancement to another position.

Other intractable realities of formal scholarly communication also contribute to its cost and slowness. The majority of academic publishers are scholarly and learned societies with very limited budgets, which makes the adoption of newer and more efficient publishing technologies difficult: The explosive growth in new research has, for many journals, led to a glut of submissions, all of which must be dealt with in some way—even early rejection costs time and money; in the current scholarly communication environment, journals that were once published only in print must now be published online (while often continuing to maintain at least some print presence, an issue that will be discussed more fully later in the book); and so forth. Not everyone agrees that these problems are necessarily permanent features of the scholarly communication landscape, and indeed system-wide solutions to them may well appear eventually. But they have not done so yet, and formal scholarly communication remains a labor- and time-intensive proposition.

Is there competition between scholarly authors?

There most certainly is, and it manifests itself in a number of ways—all of them having something to do with scholarly communication.

First of all, there is the **competition for jobs in academia**. This competition is fierce, and it becomes more so every day as graduate schools continue producing newly minted scholars and scientists in greater numbers than the job market can bear. This imbalance is caused by a number of factors. For one thing, senior faculty are often reluctant to retire, which means that existing tenure-track positions at many institutions are slow to open up—meanwhile, those very institutions continue turning out young scholars in need of work. Another factor is the generally stagnant level of funding in higher education, especially for public institutions. Static or falling budgets mean that when tenure-track positions do open up, institutions must make very difficult decisions about whether to fill them or use the salary savings elsewhere (such as to increase salaries for the remaining faculty). We have already discussed the fact that many faculty members are not on the tenure track at all, but rather are adjunct instructors (contracted on a year-by-year or semester-by-semester basis to teach particular courses). The growing number of adjunct faculty is, in part, a reflection of the growing competition for academic jobs. This increasing competition creates additional pressure on junior and aspiring faculty to publish, since a strong publication record is one of the most effective ways to set oneself apart from the competition.

This brings us to a second important aspect of competition between scholarly and scientific authors: **competition for placement in prestigious journals**. Later on we will discuss the question of how prestige is determined and some of the controversies around that issue, but for our purposes in this chapter it is important simply to understand that placement in some journals is more desirable than in others, and that the most prestigious journals turn away the great majority of article submissions. This obviously creates significant competition among scholarly and scientific authors for publication in those venues. (Of course, for authors of scholarly monographs a similar competitive dynamic exists in the marketplace for university-press publication.)

Another important aspect of competition between authors is **competition for grant funding**. This competition is especially keen in science disciplines in which research requires expensive equipment and facilities and can cost hundreds of thousands or even millions of dollars to carry out.

What all of this suggests is that while the competitive dynamic that exists between scholarly and scientific authors is not as straightforward as the one that exists between different car manufacturers or soap makers, and although scholars and scientists also frequently work together cooperatively, there are real competitive factors in the scholarly communication ecosystem that shape its dynamics significantly.

3

WHAT DOES THE SCHOLARLY COMMUNICATION MARKETPLACE LOOK LIKE?

How many scholars and scientists are publishing articles and books?

This is a reasonable question, but unfortunately a terribly difficult one to answer. It is difficult to determine how many scholarly and scientific authors are currently producing scholarly work, partly because there is no universally accepted definition of "scholarly and scientific author." Not all such authors are attached to academic institutions; some work for think tanks or research foundations, and many are research scientists employed by corporations—some of whom may publish their work and some of whom produce research outputs only for internal use by their employers. Furthermore, some scholars work independently and are not attached to institutions or organizations of any kind. (This tends to be more true of humanists than of scientists, but that is by no means a hard-and-fast rule.)

Of course, the number of publishing authors does not correspond at all directly to the number of papers published. For one thing, some authors publish many papers in a given year—but what has a far greater impact on the disconnect between the number of authors and the number of papers is the growing trend of multiple authorship. Particularly in the hard sciences, it is increasingly common for an individual article to have ten or more authors, and in some extreme cases, hundreds (or even thousands!) of authors may be credited. For obvious reasons, this practice is controversial—there is simply no way for multiple hundreds (or even dozens) of authors all to contribute meaningfully to the content of a single paper. Sometimes authorship attributions reflect a supervisory relationship, and sometimes such attributions are honorary. Whatever the explanation, the pervasive practice of attributing individual articles to more than ten authors is cause for widespread concern in the science community—though not yet sufficient concern to cause significant reform of the practice.

How much money is represented by the scholarly communication marketplace?

As of 2015, the research firm Outsell estimated that the global marketplace for publications (including journals, books, databases, etc.) in the science, technology, and math (or STM) disciplines was $26.2 billion.[1] At the same time, the research firm Simba estimated the size of the global marketplace for publications in the humanities and social science disciplines (or HSS) at $5 billion.[2] The relative size of these two numbers is noteworthy: If Outsell's and Simba's estimates are correct, the "hard" sciences have a global market share that is roughly five times that of the humanities and social sciences. The contrast is striking, but the difference itself will not come as a particular surprise to anyone who has bought or sold publications in these fields: Science journals and books tend to be vastly more expensive than those in the humanities, and publications in the "hard" sciences are often quite a bit more expensive than those in the social sciences.

Why is this discrepancy so large? The answer is complicated, and it is made more so by the fact that the voices of advocacy in the scholarly communication sphere, no matter where they come from, tend to be louder and more passionate than the voices of analysis—publishers defend their practices, advocates for change call for reform, and disinterested economic analysis can be difficult to get. Nevertheless, there are at least two possible explanations.

The first is that science publishers have monopoly control over a high-demand resource. Another way of putting this is that publishers charge a high price for STM publications because libraries will tend to buy them even at very high prices. Why do libraries do so? Because their patrons get very upset if they do not. At research universities in particular, the demand among faculty and students for access to high-quality science publications—primarily journals—is nearly insatiable, and since the faculty and students themselves do not pay the subscription fees, the high and rising cost of those subscriptions has little impact on demand for them. And since the publisher of any particular high-demand journal is selling unique content that cannot be purchased in another version from a competitor (hence the monopoly power each publisher enjoys over its publications), there is little in the way of marketplace dynamics to exert downward pressure on the price of any particular high-demand science journal. This logic would suggest that one fundamental reason books and journals in humanities cost substantially less than their counterparts in the sciences is that there is less demand for them.

A second reason is that science research tends to be more expensive than humanities research. This is not a hard-and-fast rule, of course, but it applies generally: Research that requires an expensively equipped laboratory and the assistance of a team of paid investigators costs more to undertake than research that requires a single person to consult printed books, or to conduct a survey. Not all science research takes place in the laboratory, of course, and not all humanities research takes place in the book stacks—but considering those disciplinary areas as a whole, there is a much greater distribution of low-cost research in the humanities and of high-cost research in the "hard" sciences.

This observation raises another question, though: Since the researcher herself is not having her costs offset by the publisher of her article, why would the relatively expensive nature of science research necessarily lead to a relatively high price for science publications? In other words, it may cost more to study DNA than to study the poems of John Donne, but does it actually cost more to prepare an article on DNA for publication than to do the same for a paper on Donne? The answer is yes, at least in many cases. The Donne article will likely consist almost entirely of text, which is relatively inexpensive to prepare for publication. In contrast, a DNA article (or a histology article or an oncology article) is likely to involve multiple color images, which are expensive to prepare for publication. The vetting of an article in the hard sciences (particularly in medicine) may also be quite a bit more involved and expensive than that needed for an article that makes a literary argument. But how much of the price differential between science journals and humanities journals can be accounted for by this difference? That is a more difficult question.

Again, it is important to point out that these variables exist on a variety of continua: The scholarly and scientific publishing ecosystem is not populated entirely by medical studies and literary arguments, and some social science studies might be more expensive to publish than some hard science studies. After all is said and done, it seems likely that the most important single factor in the cost differential between STEM and HSS publications is the marketplace dynamic of supply and demand. No research library can afford not to subscribe to the top journals in the disciplines that are areas of strategic focus for that library's host institution; thus, the publishers of those top journals can charge very high prices for them—and they do.

How many scholarly publishers are there?

The definition of "scholarly publisher" is somewhat fuzzy, and there is no centralized global directory of scholarly publishers, making it difficult to calculate any kind of exact figure in response to this question. A published estimate from 2006 put the global number of scholarly journal publishers at 657,[3] and as of this writing Wikipedia lists 157 university presses worldwide.[4] But not all scholarly book publishers are university presses, and not all book publishers can be cleanly characterized as either "scholarly" or "non-scholarly." To give one example of the implications of this ambiguity for a meaningful survey of global scholarly publishing, consider the fact that a 2007 analysis found that in India alone there were over 12,000 book publishers registered with the International Standard Book Number (ISBN) office for that country.[5] For all of these reasons, it is probably not possible to know exactly how many scholarly publishers there are at any given moment.

How many books and journals do they publish?

These numbers are a bit easier to establish. In 2014, there were roughly 28,000 scholarly and scientific peer-reviewed journals being published. In recent years, the number of journals has increased by about 2.5% per year.[6] However, these numbers are becoming less meaningful as the journal ecosystem changes. For example, the rise of mega-journals, some of which publish tens of thousands of articles per year, means that counting unique journal titles no longer helps us understand the journal marketplace in the way it once did. For example, to count *PLOS ONE* (which publishes between 25,000 and 30,000 articles per year) and the *American Journal of Obstetrics and Gynecology* (which publishes, depending on how one counts, between 100 and 200 articles per year) each as a single journal risks greatly distorting one's idea of the size of the journal literature. (For more discussion of mega-journals and how they work, see Chapter 12.)

Another confounding factor is the rise of the "predatory" or deceptive journal. This problem will be discussed more fully in Chapter 13, but for our purposes here it is worth noting that since fake journals (and even fake publishing operations) can be set up very quickly and easily online—and even more quickly taken down when they are exposed—keeping track of them can be quite difficult, and counting them is problematic both logistically and conceptually. Which journals should we assume are real (and therefore count as part of the journal marketplace) and which ones might be fake? These questions are relatively easy to answer at the margins, but there exists a large area of ambiguity as well.

As for scholarly books: While current industry-wide data are somewhat hard to come by, a study by the *Humanities Indicators* project (affiliated with the American Academy of Arts & Sciences) found that in 2013 roughly 120,000 new books had been published across all scholarly and scientific disciplines: 54,000 in the humanities, 13,000 in the behavioral and social sciences, 7,000 in engineering, 8,000 in medicine, 13,000 in the natural sciences, and 26,000 in fields designated as "other." Furthermore, the study found slow but relatively steady growth in academic book publishing during the five-year study period leading up to 2013.[7]

One of the things that makes it difficult to say how many scholarly books are published each year is that when doing so, one must resolve ambiguities around what one is counting. Some data sets will count hardback, paperback, and e-book editions of the same title separately, particularly if the electronic or paperback version is published some time later than the original hardback.

Another ambiguity lies in the nature of the word "scholarly" or "academic." Particularly in humanistic disciplines, the line between a scholarly and non-scholarly work of history or biography may be quite fuzzy—whereas in fields such as medicine, for example, the difference between a clinical and a popular book about cancer will usually be much more apparent.

4

WHAT IS SCHOLARLY PUBLISHING AND HOW DOES IT WORK?

What is the difference between scholarly communication and scholarly publishing?

As discussed in Chapter 2, scholars communicate with each other in a wide variety of ways, all of which exist on a spectrum of formality. At the informal end of the spectrum are the conversations that scholars have with each other—at work, in the hallways at conferences, on the phone, or by e-mail. Somewhere in the middle of the spectrum are document-based communications like conference posters, graduate theses and dissertations, the online sharing of unpublished article manuscripts and preprints, and blog postings. At the formal end of the spectrum are publications like journal articles, monographs, white papers, and conference presentations.

Obviously, the closer a mode of scholarly communication gets to the informal end of the spectrum, the less likely it is to be officially published in any way. Publishers begin to get involved only as scholarly communication moves to the formal end of the spectrum—a conference poster may get published, either in its original form or (more likely) as the basis for an article; a white paper created for in-house use by a foundation may be packaged more formally and made available to the public, either for free or for sale; a dissertation may be revised and turned into a formally published scholarly monograph. And documents that are created specifically for publication will typically be submitted to a publisher immediately upon completion.

So the answer to the question *What is the difference between scholarly communication and scholarly publishing?* is that scholarly publishing is a subset of scholarly communication. All scholarly publishing is scholarly communication, but only some scholarly communication consists in formal (or even informal) publication.

But this begs another question: What is it that scholarly publishers actually do?

What do scholarly publishers do?

Historically, scholarly publishers have provided four very important categories of service to authors and to the reading public:

1. They have *selected submitted materials* for quality and relevance.
2. They have *provided editorial services* and thereby worked to improve and refine the author's work.
3. They have made the final versions of the vetted and edited materials *available to the public*—usually at a price.
4. They *provide branding and marketing for the author's work*, conferring a marker of prestige on the document in question and helping to bring it to the attention of the author's colleagues (and maybe even the general public).

Each of these represents a way in which we say that publishers "add value" to the work of scholars: As it emerges from the author's pen, the work may or may not be relevant to a particular field; it may or may not be clearly written or follow very well the conventions of grammar and punctuation; it will almost never have been formatted and typeset in an attractive way consistent with the presentation of a formal journal or printed book; and it will not be easily distinguishable from unvetted manuscripts. The publisher is said to "add value" when:

- It selects one article or book manuscript over another (thus saving its readers from having to read and separately evaluate hundreds or thousands of articles or manuscripts in the search for relevant and reliable information).
- It improves editorially upon the original manuscript version of the article or book (clearing up infelicities of language, tightening the document's structure, etc.)
- It makes the document discoverable by and widely available to readers.
- It certifies the work as reliable and of high quality.

We will look at each of these functions in turn, and consider some of the ways in which they have changed in recent years—and, in some cases, continue to change.

The *selectivity function* of publishers is one that remains important both to authors and to readers, and of the broad functions outlined above it is the one that has probably changed the least over the past few decades. Imagine if all of the book manuscripts submitted to publishers were automatically accepted and published regardless of their quality or their relevance to particular fields—one would never know, when picking up a book, whether one was about to read nonsense or carefully considered scholarship. When accessing an issue of a journal of pediatric medicine, one would have no way of knowing whether the articles contained in it had anything to do with pediatric medicine, or any reliable grounding in solid scientific practice; some probably would, and some would not. None of this is to say, of course, that monographs published by university presses or articles published by scholarly journals are always of top intellectual quality, or that the processes of formal publication are sufficiently rigorous to absolve readers of the duties of critical reading and judgment. But one of the important functions that publishers have historically performed for readers is that of giving them a rough cut of scholarship. A reader may not be able to say to himself "I read it in *The Lancet*, and therefore I know it to be true"; however, a reader can assume that if he sees an article in *The Lancet*, it has gone through a serious degree of review by scientists who know the field, and it is therefore likely to be relevant to the field of medicine and its content will be worth at least taking seriously.

The *editorial function* of scholarly publishing is another one that continues to be valued both by authors and by readers. An article or book may contain highly useful and innovative information, and yet be poorly organized or written in a style that is unnecessarily unclear. The author may not be gifted (or even fully fluent) in the language in which the article or book is written, and the text may need significant revisions before it will be acceptably readable (revisions that will then need to be reviewed by the author to make sure they have not changed the meaning of the text). Once the content itself has been rendered acceptable, its format will need to be adjusted to fit with the publication. Every journal or book publisher has a "house style" with regard to text and citation formatting, to which all manuscripts will need to be adapted so that readers can count on a certain amount of consistency from article to article or book to book. If the text includes photographs, charts, or other graphical content, there are issues of image size and resolution to consider (not to mention copyright issues, which can be complex). Someone will usually have to double-check the validity of links in the text and in the citations. These are only some of the many editorial functions that have been and continue to be performed by publishers.

Selection and editing have been important aspects of scholarly publishing nearly from the beginning, and both remain important today, even after several decades of radical change in the ways information is generated and distributed for public use. However, those changes have had a much more significant impact on the third way in which publishers have traditionally added value: *making scholarship discoverable* and widely available to readers and researchers.

For centuries, discovering the existence of particular documents was difficult: Only the very privileged had access to catalogues, and those catalogues were rudimentary at best and always out of date. As printing and publishing technologies advanced, it became easier for readers to learn about the existence of particular books and articles, and of course today we have the Internet with its very powerful search engines, which have created an unprecedented richness of discoverability. However, learning that a document exists is not the same thing as having access to it. During the print era, publishers made documents publicly accessible by printing multiple copies, distributing them physically, and providing the copies for sale. Having bought a copy of a document, one could extend its accessibility by lending it to others—or by creating new copies of it (legally or not).

Obviously, it is this aspect of publishing that has changed most radically with the advent of the Internet. No author needs to rely on publishers anymore to make her work available to a very large readership (although making it available is not the same thing as making it discoverable, as we will discuss further below). The Internet represents a set of interlocking technologies that are built on such game-changing functionalities as high-speed searching of text and metadata, automatic copying of documents, and virtually instantaneous transmission of text and images, making online documents both radically more discoverable than ever before and infinitely more shareable. Not since the invention of the telephone has a technological innovation had such a seismic impact on human communication—and one small manifestation of that impact lies in the fact that no one really needs publishers anymore in order to make their intellectual work available to billions of people.

While the functions of selectivity, editorial review, and quality control remain highly valued both by readers (as evidenced by their continued willingness to buy access to formal scholarly publications) and by authors (as evidenced by their continued willingness to submit their work for formal publication instead of simply making it freely available online), the value that publishers offer as distributors of content has been significantly undermined.

A fourth very important function of publishers is that of *prestige marking and marketing*. For the author, to have an article published in a particular journal or a book published with a particular publishing house is to have the prestige of that venue attached to one's work, and the publisher's marketing muscle flexed on the work's behalf. The former is an exceptionally important function for scholars, who generally need more than just to make their work available to readers—they need a quick and intuitive way to signal to readers that their work has been vetted and found to be worthy. Getting one's article published in *New England Journal of Medicine* or one's book published by Harvard University Press sends that message very effectively. Placing one's work with a publisher also helps to ensure that the work will be found by readers—an especially important consideration in the context of an ever-more-cluttered Internet. It is one thing to make one's work technically available, and quite another to ensure that it is actually found by those who might want to read it.

What is peer review and how does it work?

Peer review is a very important concept in the world of scholarly communication. It describes a system of intellectual quality control whereby one or more of an author's peers and colleagues are invited to review her work prior to publication and provide critical input. This part of the publication process typically takes place after the author has submitted her work for consideration and it has passed a general editorial first cut: The editor has examined it sufficiently to determine that its content is within scope, it is reasonably well written, and it seems to present significant and valid scholarly or scientific arguments.

Input by the author's peers is solicited, in part, because no editor has either the breadth of knowledge or the time to comprehensively critique every paper submitted, particularly in journals of relatively broad scope (like *Nature*, for example, as opposed to the *Journal of Bone and Joint Surgery*). Peer review is also important because it provides an additional layer of presumably disinterested oversight. Traditionally, peer review is "blind," which means that the author does not know who has reviewed her article; sometimes it is "double blind," meaning that identifying information about the author or authors is stripped from the article manuscript and the reviewers themselves therefore do not know who the author is. (Nevertheless, the disinterestedness of peer reviewers is not always perfect: In smaller disciplines it may be relatively easy to guess who has written the article one is reviewing, and it is not always easy to put one's own biases aside when reviewing the work of a colleague who is obviously working from a different, and perhaps conflicting, set of assumptions or values.)

Having been invited to review a manuscript, reviewers will typically respond to a series of questions after reading it. These may include:

- Is the article within scope for this journal?
- Is it original?
- Does it address an important research question?
- Is its methodology sound?
- Do its conclusions follow from the data presented?
- Is it clearly and cogently written?

And so forth. The reviewer is then usually asked to make a recommendation as to whether the manuscript should be published as it is, should be revised and resubmitted, or should be rejected. These comments and recommendations are then taken into account by the editor, who makes a final publishing decision. If the recommendation is to revise and resubmit, the original reviewer will often be asked to review the revised version as well.

In recent years, with the growth of the open access movement and concomitant increases in interest in openness generally, there has been growing interest in open peer review. Open peer review refers to various arrangements by which authors and reviewers are known to each other and the reviewing process happens openly between them, and often even publicly.

Another recent variation on the traditional peer-review arrangement is called "post-publication" peer review. Under this system, the article is accepted and published with minimal or no peer review, and review then takes place afterwards and becomes part of the public record regarding the article. The reviewers may be self-selected volunteers, or may be invited either by the author or by the journal publisher.

Peer reviewers usually work without direct pay. In most cases they are academics and scientists employed at academic or research institutions for whom this kind of participation in the scholarly communication ecosystem is built into their job expectations, and it is seen as part of their professional duty. They review the work of others with the expectation that others will step up and do the same for their papers when asked to do so. The voluntary nature of peer review creates challenges, as one might expect: Not everyone agrees to do it when asked, and—even worse— not everyone who agrees to do it follows through in a timely way, or at all. Managing the peer-review process is one of the most important duties of a journal editor, and it can also be one of the most frustrating and onerous.

The phrase "peer-reviewed journal" is one that will recur throughout this book and that is often invoked during conversations about scholarly communication. In most scholarly and scientific disciplines, publishing in peer-reviewed journals is essential to academic advancement. But scholarly book publishers employ peer review as well, in much the same way that journals do. In addition, these publishers will often use committees to review book proposals and provide input as to which of them should be accepted.

Does peer review actually work?

Yes—though like every other system that human beings create, it works imperfectly. In recent years there has been growing controversy around the effectiveness, fairness, and efficiency of traditional models of peer review, and those controversies are largely responsible for the growth of alternative models of review and publishing. There seems to be wide agreement on the basic idea that science and scholarship need to be open to scrutiny and quality control, that editors alone are not capable of providing all the scrutiny required, and that an author's colleagues are probably the ones best placed to provide the input and quality control needed. But there is far less agreement on what does and does not work in traditional peer review, or about the desirability of replacing traditional peer review with something new—and among those who agree that traditional peer review needs to be replaced, there is not yet a consensus as to what should replace it or exactly how it should be improved. This controversy is, itself, part of the normal functioning of science and scholarship.

However, it is worth noting that even when the traditional system of peer review functions as intended, the system itself has its critics. It certainly slows down the process of publication, and even when functioning at its best, the reliability and effectiveness of peer review depend on the availability, attentiveness, and objectivity of reviewers in the relevant field. To the degree that reviewers are experienced and established scholars and scientists, there exists a danger that their work as peer reviewers will tend to marginalize innovation and new thinking. And as more than one scholar has discovered, once one demonstrates one's ability and willingness to provide a useful and reliable review (and to do so on a deadline), the review invitations quickly multiply.

What happens when peer review fails to function as it should?

Peer review is an example of a system of trust: It only works as intended if its participants can be relied upon to represent their identities, affiliations, and expertise accurately, and to carry out their duties diligently and in good faith.

Given the sheer number of scholarly articles and books submitted for publication each year, and the fact that in many cases these are reviewed by multiple peer reviewers, it is inevitable that abuses of that trust will occur. Such abuses may take a number of forms.

One example is when peer reviewers fail to disclose conflicts of interest. If a reviewer has, for example, a lucrative consulting relationship with a corporation whose product is under examination in the study being reviewed, this might affect the way in which the reviewer assesses the study's quality and findings. If the reviewer is herself in the process of doing a study that seems to point toward a different conclusion from the one in the article she has been asked to review, that too may create a conflict of interest (depending on her personal investment in the outcome of her project).

Peer-review failure might also arise from philosophical conflict or disagreement. This is a particular risk because those invited to review a paper on a given scholarly or scientific topic are likely to be researchers working in the same field as the author, and who may be in competition with that author for resources or may disagree with the author's conclusions for reasons not entirely related to the evidence presented in the paper under review. It is often difficult to put one's own biases aside when assessing the work of others who disagree, and this can undermine one's objectivity as a reviewer of others' work.

Sometimes the failure of peer review is much simpler: Peer review is promised but simply does not happen. This is a particularly noteworthy problem among "predatory" journals (which are discussed in more detail in Chapter 13) but can happen with any journal. Sometimes it is not the journal that promises without delivering, but the reviewer himself—every editor of a peer-reviewed journal can share multiple horror stories about scholars who accept review assignments but never fulfill them, leaving not only the journal but also the author hanging, sometimes literally for years.

And, of course, it is also true that even when all of the mechanics of peer review are carried out faithfully, no reviewer is perfect. The most well-intentioned and unbiased reviewers may miss errors of logic or study design, instances of plagiarism, or any number of other flaws intrinsic to the scholarship itself.

In short, there is no question that peer review is an imperfect system. That it remains so central to the scholarly communication enterprise is a testament not to its perfection, but to the lack (so far) of a widely accepted alternative system of vetting and certification.

What is "retraction" and why does it happen?

A scholarly paper is retracted if, after publication, very serious flaws are discovered in it. In some cases, the flaws may result from unconscionably shoddy scholarly or scientific work—obviously, a major purpose of peer review is to detect such flaws in submitted papers well before they are prepared for publication, allowing the editor either to reject the paper or to insist on substantial revision.

However, not even the most thorough and conscientious peer review in the world will catch every fundamental flaw in every paper. This is especially the case when the problems with the paper do not arise from inattention or poor reasoning, but rather from conscious and deliberate deception. A researcher who simply fabricates his data, or who misrepresents a cheap and sloppy experimental design as rigorous and painstaking, is not likely to have his deception revealed in the course of peer review—after all, the reviewer has no way of knowing what actually happened in the laboratory, cannot fully replicate the study, and may not have full access to the raw data set on which the study is based. This kind of problem may not be brought to light until another researcher tries (and fails) to replicate the original study's findings using the same methodology, or until a whistleblower from the lab makes an accusation. Recent movements toward making raw data accessible both to reviewers and to readers are helping to solve this problem to some degree.

What all of this means is that formally published papers are not usually retracted just because they are found to be flawed or because later studies have resulted in contradictory findings. Retraction usually signals that something is seriously and fundamentally wrong with the paper, and very often the problem identified is one arising from scholarly or scientific bad faith. For this reason, retraction is not undertaken lightly.

Scholarly books can be withdrawn from the marketplace as well, when they are found to be based on fraudulent data, fabricated narratives, or substantial plagiarism. However, the word "retraction" is (for some reason) not usually used in the context of books; books are usually "withdrawn."

What is the "replication crisis"?

This is a term that has recently come into broad usage, describing a growing concern in the scholarly and scientific community over the validity of much published research. It is also sometimes referred to as the "reproducibility crisis."

It is a hallmark of the scientific method that research results should be replicable or reproducible—that is, we take it as given that if a study is designed well and carried out conscientiously and in good faith, it should yield the same (or substantially the same) results every time it is conducted under the same conditions and controlling for the same variables. If a published study is replicated and the results are considerably different, that casts doubt on the validity of the study that was published.

In recent years there has been growing concern in the scientific community about the number of published studies that do not seem to stand up to this basic test. In 2015, one published analysis found that roughly two-thirds of the studies in three high-ranking psychology journals failed the replication test—in other words, when two-thirds of those studies were repeated, they did not yield significant findings even though the published studies had claimed such findings.[1] That this should be the case in the field of psychology is perhaps not completely shocking, since psychology (along with other social sciences) attempts to study things that are extremely difficult to measure, or the very existence of which may be controversial (emotions, attitudes, the mind, etc.). However, reproducibility levels in the "hard" sciences are coming under increasing scrutiny as well: A recent survey published in the journal *Nature* found that of the scientists surveyed, more than 70% had attempted to replicate others' experiments and failed, and that more than half of them had failed to replicate their own earlier work. Fifty-two percent of the survey respondents answered the question "Is there a reproducibility crisis?" with "Yes, a significant crisis."[2]

One might well ask whether the problems we are currently seeing with reproducibility in science are of recent origin or have been bubbling along for many years. It would take significant research to answer that question in a rigorous way, but developments in scholarly communication during the past few decades give reason to believe that the problem has become more severe in recent years. For one thing, there has been a huge explosion in the amount of science published since World War II.[3] Even if the proportion of good science to bad has remained unchanged during that period, the increase in the sheer amount of bad science in circulation would be a significant problem.

For another, during that same period there has been a concomitant explosion in the number of journals published.[4] As the field of scientific journals becomes more crowded, the need grows for those journals to differentiate themselves—which means, among other things, publishing high-impact articles. This creates an incentive (or, rather, strengthens the already existing incentive) to be less critical in accepting papers that tout surprising or exciting findings.

Unsurprisingly, the replication crisis is a matter of some controversy. Some suggest that the problems of replicability in the social sciences constitute evidence that those sciences are themselves not really science; others argue that the implications of the crisis for biomedicine are more dire because they involve life-and-death issues more often than the social sciences do—not to mention much, much more money.[5] Few seem to believe that the crisis is not real, though, and there is general concern that if the crisis is not addressed, it threatens to undermine the public's confidence in science (and maybe not entirely without reason).

How has the work of publishers changed since the advent of the Internet?

During the print era, publishers took submissions of articles, subjected those articles to editorial scrutiny (often involving a layer of review by one or more of the author's peers as well), and either accepted or rejected the articles based on editorial assessments of the relevance and quality of the work and also on counsel from peer reviewers as to the work's quality and importance. Once accepted, articles were further edited before being formatted and typeset for publication, then bundled with other articles into journal issues, printed, and distributed to subscribers. Scholarly book publishers did much the same thing using some of the same processes, only the end results of these processes were bound and printed monographs or collections rather than issues of journals. In both cases, publishers have also worked to maintain the strength of their brands and to market their publications to potential buyers.

In the digital era, publishers still do virtually all of the things they did in the print era, and also a large and growing number of new things. For example, although the demand for printed copies of journal issues has been declining for years, it will not reach zero in the foreseeable future, due in part to a continued love of the print format in the developed world and (more importantly) the uneven accessibility of the Internet in the developing world. This means that even as publishers become online entities offering digital information products, many of them are under pressure to continue being print-based entities offering physical copies of their products as well.

What does becoming an online publisher entail? In addition to selecting appropriate content and providing editorial services, it also generally means creating and curating an online archive of past issues (or paying a third-party service provider to do so), supporting online access to content on an ongoing basis, complying with new rules and regulations imposed by government and other funding agencies (none of which existed during the print era), controlling versions of articles, marketing new and backlist publications to the public, and monitoring threats of hacking and large-scale piracy, among many other things.

The archiving issue is particularly worth noting. In the print era, publishers were not generally expected to act as permanent archives for what they published—books went out of print, a journal issue was superseded quickly by the following issue, and publishers continued producing new content. The publisher did not serve as the permanent archival host on which society would rely for access to what they published—that role was largely filled by libraries. But once a publication moves online, readers expect to be able to find it there in perpetuity.

Of course, the fact that publishers do all of these many things does not necessarily mean that everyone agrees they should do them—either that all of those things need to be done or that those things that do need to be done ought to be done by publishers. This brings us to the next question:

Do we really need publishers in order for scholarship to advance—and if so, why?

This is a controversial question in the twenty-first century, for a number of reasons.

Since at least the 1960s, there has been growing concern over three important developments in the world of scholarly communication: the growing cost of scholarly journals (especially in the science, technology, engineering, and mathematics—or STEM—disciplines), the flat or declining funding of academic libraries, and concomitant declines in library purchases of scholarly monographs as libraries have shifted money away from book purchases in order to avoid cutting journal subscriptions. Each of these developments will be treated in more depth elsewhere in the book; for now, it is important to understand that these developments (among others) have led to a growing sense of discontent with scholarly publishers, especially among librarians, but also among some members of the academic faculty. With the advent of the Internet and thus of a new ability to copy and distribute documents at virtually no incremental unit cost, some members of the scholarly ecosystem have raised increasing doubts as to the necessity of publishers at all—while others have raised doubts about whether we still need libraries.

When considering this issue, it is important to recognize that the universe of scholarly publishers consists of two very different broad categories of organization: for-profit commercial publishers (such as Reed-Elsevier, Taylor & Francis, and John Wiley & Sons) and nonprofit publishing enterprises that are usually organs of educational institutions or scholarly and scientific societies (such as university presses and journal publishers like the Seismological Society of America and the American Historical Association). There are also publishers that do not fit perfectly into either category: Oxford University Press, for example, is both a university press and a multinational corporation with gross revenues in the hundreds of millions of dollars per year, while the American Chemical Society is technically a nonprofit society publisher that also generates hundreds of millions of dollars in annual revenues by publishing high-priced journals and databases. But these are outliers, and most of the publishing activity that takes place in the scholarly ecosystem fits fairly comfortably within the rubric of "commercial for-profit publishing" and "nonprofit institutional or society publishing."

One of the factors complicating the question of whether publishers are still needed in the ecosystem of scholarly communication is the fact that scholarly and scientific societies not only charge for access to their published content, but also use the revenues generated thereby to provide services to their members. For many societies, a subscription to the house journal is provided as a benefit of membership; for others, subscription fees underwrite other organizational activities and yield member benefits such as discounted registration fees at annual meetings.

But none of this answers the question of whether we need publishers in order for scholarship to advance. The answer to that question is (of course!) complicated, in part by the fact that not everyone agrees on the value of those things that publishers do, or on what the proper roles and functions of publishers are. Publishers provide one set of services to authors and a very different one to readers (and to the libraries who often act as brokers of access on behalf of readers), so it may be a good idea to begin answering this question by posing a different one: Why do scholars submit their work to publishers and how do they choose between them? The first of those questions was addressed in Chapter 2, but the second is worth addressing here.

How do scholars decide whether and where to publish?

Scholars will be motivated by any number of different factors when deciding whether, where, and how to publish their work, but among the most important of these—especially for those who are seeking tenure—is prestige. In order to secure ongoing employment (in the form of tenure), academics generally need to publish in venues that are recognized by their colleagues as highly reputable and selective. Publishing an article in a highly respected peer-reviewed journal, or publishing a book with a big university press, signals to your peers that your work has been taken seriously and deemed worthy by those who know what good scholarly work in your field looks like. Since your academic peers are the ones who vote on your tenure bid (but probably do not have time to read for themselves and critically evaluate everything you have written), having an article published in *Nature* or *Lancet* or a book published by the University of Chicago Press has real implications for your ability to stay employed in academia. For that reason, this kind of academic "branding" is tremendously important and it drives authors' publishing choices to a significant degree.

But scholars communicate for other important reasons as well, of course. It is hard to imagine a scholar publishing without the hope that others will read what she has written, and the desire to be widely read may conflict with the desire to publish in a prestigious venue. While high-profile journals like *Nature* and *Lancet* have relatively large readerships, many other scholarly journals—even well-regarded ones—do not, and the readership of most journals is limited to its subscriber base, which, even if relatively large, will necessarily be limited. Scholars who are more interested in the broadest possible readership than in prestige are likely to publish in venues that are open and accessible to the general public, such as blogs, free online publications, and open access journals (a growing number of which are becoming prestigious publication venues in their own right). And it is also worth noting that an individual scholar will publish different types of writing in different venues, depending on its purpose: opinion pieces in a professional newsletter or a personal or professional blog, research articles in peer-reviewed journals, and so forth.

Another important venue for publishing (although here the word "publish" may not quite fit) is the preprint repository.[6] For several decades now, authors have found various ways of widely sharing preliminary versions of their work prior to formal publication—partly in an effort to establish publicly the priority of their discoveries and ideas, and partly as a way of troubleshooting and refining their work before submitting it for formal publication. In the 1960s such sharing became common in some disciplines, with scholars sharing their drafts by mail; in Chapter 2 we mentioned an online archive of preprints in the area of high-energy physics that was established at the

Los Alamos National Laboratory and came to be called the arXiv[7]; that service has since come to embrace other quantitative science disciplines as well, and it moved to the library at Cornell University in 2011. A similar preprint service for the biological sciences, called the bioRxiv, was established in 2013.[8] This kind of scholarly communication, though not hidden from the public and fully accessible by anyone interested, nevertheless takes place largely outside of public notice and occupies a sort of middle region between conversation among peers and colleagues and formal publication.

When we get into the topic of institutional repositories (IRs), which generally contain a wide variety of works in a wide variety of disciplines, some of them having been formally published and some not, we get into an even grayer area of "publishing." IRs will be discussed in more detail in Chapter 12 on open access.

So, do we actually need publishers in this day and age?

Whether they are commercial, for-profit enterprises or institutional, nonprofit ones, scholarly publishers are kept in business by two things: a constant flow of submitted content from authors, and a constant flow of revenues from readers, brokers, or institutions. (In some cases, both content and revenue come from authors, or at least from the author side of the equation—for further discussion, see Chapter 12.) Without both content and revenue, the publisher cannot continue to do its work.

The fact that scholarly publishing continues to be a more or less thriving business, then, suggests that both authors and readers still see a real need for publishers. Authors want not only to make their work widely available (which, again, they can now accomplish without recourse to formal publication) but also to give it the imprimatur of quality and relevance that a reputable journal or book publisher provides. Readers want access, and very often access is only available in return for payments made to publishers or publishers' agents. So the most obvious answer to the question "Do we really need publishers?" is yes, based on the demonstrable behavior of those who derive direct benefit from the work that publishers do.

But there is another possible answer to this question: It may be that we actually no longer need publishers, but that neither scholarly and scientific authors nor paying readers have yet caught up to this reality. It is possible that authors submit their work to publishers not because they truly need publishers' services, but rather because they are ignorant of alternatives that they would find equally acceptable if they only knew about them. Or it may be that authors do know about these alternatives, but are not yet convinced of their acceptability and need to be educated accordingly. As for readers, the situation is somewhat different: As long as publishers are either the copyright holders in or the possessors of exclusive distribution licenses for scholarly content, readers have few legal options other than buying it from publishers or relying on brokers, such as libraries, to purchase it on their behalf.

Interestingly, this means that the ongoing submission behavior of authors may be a more reliable measure of the ongoing necessity of publishers than is the purchasing behavior of readers and libraries. Authors may believe erroneously that they need publishers, but to the degree that publishers continue to have control over content, readers have little choice (within the law, anyway) but to avail themselves of publishers' services if they want access to content. Of course, one might easily argue that the persistence of this arrangement reflects inertia or an unhealthy market power on the part of publishers rather than real need. Opinions on this question are mixed, and that disagreement is at the heart of some of the controversies we will be discussing later in the book.

What is the role of societies in scholarly communication?

Professional, scientific, and scholarly associations and societies (often referred to collectively as "learned societies," particularly in the United Kingdom, but which we will refer to in this book by the shorthand designation "societies") fulfill a number of important roles for scholars and scientists, and several of those roles have a direct bearing on scholarly communication.

For context, it is important to understand that for many if not most working scholars and scientists, there is a stronger feeling of identity with, and loyalty to, their professional disciplines than to the academic institutions in which they work.[9] This is understandable: If you are a research biologist working at the University of Texas, you will remain a Longhorn for only as long as you are at Texas—but you will be a biologist for your entire career. Furthermore, you are likely to have much more in common professionally with a biologist at a different university than with a literature professor at your own university. To the degree that these things are true, you are likely to seek out opportunities for networking, collaboration, and socialization with biologists from other academic institutions. You will tend to read the same journal articles, attend the same conferences, and follow the same professional blogs as your disciplinary colleagues around the world.

All of this goes some way toward explaining why societies emerged hundreds of years ago, and why they persist: a well-run society helps meet a number of keenly felt needs for many working scholars and scientists.

Like any organization, societies must have revenue streams in order to do their work. One mechanism for generating revenue is to charge membership fees, which virtually all societies do. However, in order to attract scholars and scientists in the early stages of their careers, when they are beginning to form alliances that will shape their future work lives but also when money is often tight, societies feel pressure to keep membership fees low.

Another important revenue stream for societies tends to be an annual conference of some kind, which also serves as an important venue for scholars and scientists to network with each other, interview for jobs, and present their work publicly. Again, though, there is significant pressure on the society to keep conference costs low so that those who are early in their careers (or working at institutions that provide little travel support) will be able to attend.

This brings us to a third common source of revenue for societies: journal publishing. As mentioned in Chapter 1, the earliest scholarly journals were society publications. Society publishing remains a vitally important segment of the scholarly communication marketplace, providing readers with specialized scholarly content in an enormous variety of fields and disciplines while providing authors with valuable venues in which to have their work certified as quality scholarship and to make that work available to interested readers. One of the interesting things about society journal publishing is that many societies use the revenues from journal subscriptions in order to partially underwrite the costs of membership and conference attendance, thus making both of those services more affordable to their members.

Why are so many society journals being licensed or sold to commercial publishers?

While a great many societies publish journals, most societies are not heavily staffed with publishing professionals, and are not well positioned to benefit from economies of scale—while a few societies publish lots of journals, most publish only one or a handful. This reality tends to limit the revenue potential of journal publishing for most societies. It also offers an opportunity to publishers that do have access to economies of scale, not to mention significant capital and staff resources. In recent years it has become increasingly common for such publishers (notably including Wiley, Elsevier, and Oxford University Press) to reach out to society publishers and offer to take over the publishing of their journals and share the revenues. In many cases, these publishers can confidently promise a net increase in revenues to the society, while also taking a significant workload off the society's staff.

The upside to an arrangement like this can be significant for the society. The downside of such arrangements is experienced by the journal's subscribers: Almost invariably, a society's sale of its journal to a commercial publisher results in a significant increase in the subscription price.[10]

5

WHAT IS THE ROLE
OF COPYRIGHT?

Why do we have copyright law?

Although there have been various laws throughout history designed to regulate publishing, modern copyright law has its clearest roots in the Statute of Anne, established in England in 1709. This act of Parliament was intended to stop "Printers, Booksellers, and other Persons" from "Printing, Reprinting, and Publishing, or causing to be Printed, Reprinted, and Published Books, and other Writings, without the Consent of the Authors or Proprietors of such Books and Writings, to their very great Detriment, and too often to the Ruin of them and their Families."[1] The basic function of this statute was to give authors the sole right to say whether and by whom their original works could be printed and reprinted; the author held that right for fourteen years, and then (if the author was still alive) for another fourteen years, after which point the work would enter the public domain and no longer be subject to copyright restrictions.

American copyright laws began emerging at the state level during the years prior to the ratification of the Constitution, but copyright was made a matter of national law with Article 1, Section 8, Clause 8 of that document, which empowers Congress "to promote the Progress of

Science and useful Arts, by securing for limited Times to Authors and Inventors the exclusive Right to their respective Writings and Discoveries."[2] Ever since its adoption in the United States, there has been controversy over the appropriate balance between the rights of authors and the rights of the general public. Given that the stated purpose of copyright is to "promote the Progress of Science and useful Arts," is that purpose better served by giving authors tighter control over their work (thus giving them more opportunity to profit from it, thereby encouraging them to come up with more and better work), or by giving the public more opportunities to distribute, reuse, and expand upon the work (thus giving everyone more opportunity to read the work and build upon it, thereby creating new work themselves)?

This controversy has not been settled, and the wholesale shift of the information economy from the physical realm, where copying and redistribution were relatively laborious and expensive propositions, to a networked online environment where copying and redistribution are extremely easy and cheap, has only complicated it further. Among the many things that this ongoing controversy means is that not everyone agrees, in fact, that we need copyright law— or, at least, that copyright law should continue as currently configured. Even among those who support American copyright law, for example, in its broad current configuration, there are widespread concerns about some of its details, such as the very long term of copyright protection currently granted under the law: as of 1998, for works by individual authors the term is the life of the author plus seventy years, or ninety-five years after initial publication, whichever comes first, though the rules are different for works published before 1978. It is complicated.[3]

However, when it comes to scholarly communication, there are deeper concerns about the appropriate application of copyright law itself. Given that so much scholarly and scientific endeavor is underwritten by public funds, does it make sense to grant copyright to the authors of the resulting works—or does copyright in such works rightly belong with the public who funded the underlying research? Some suggest that even when scholarly and scientific work is privately underwritten, it is not right to treat knowledge itself like a commodity and grant access to it only to those who can afford to pay; from this perspective, the products of scholarship should be the common property of all. What better way to "promote the progress of science and the useful arts" than to make scientific and artistic works as broadly accessible and reusable as possible? According to this view, scholarly communication is very different from, say, the production of commercial films, novels, or popular journalism, and should be subject to different norms when it comes to public accessibility.

Those who support traditional copyright protections for scholarship might respond that authors should have the right to exercise at least some limited control over the reappropriation, revision, and alteration of their original work, and that this may be particularly important in humanistic areas of scholarship, where personal interpretation and styles of expression may be centrally important.[4] According to this view, even if scholarly authors do not generally depend on copyright to provide them with direct income (most of them having been paid an institutional salary while producing their works of scholarship), they still have a reasonable expectation to maintain some degree of control over their original creations.

Clearly, these are complicated and vexed questions, and they are becoming more so as the scholarly communication ecosystem itself becomes more complex. Questions about copyright and licensing will come up again later, in the chapter on open access and related issues.

Are all published works under copyright?

No. There are two broad categories of written and recorded work that are not subject to copyright: those that were once under copyright but are now in the public domain, and those that are not subject to copyright at all.

Not very many categories of documents fall under the latter designation, but one very important example of non-copyrightable documents is those produced by the U.S. government. According to U.S. copyright law, "a 'work of the United States Government' is a work prepared by an officer or employee of the United States Government as part of that person's official duties."[5] Such works are not subject to copyright but are in the public domain—meaning that they can be reused in any way a member of the public sees fit. They can be copied and redistributed freely, authors can create derivative works based on them without having to seek anyone's permission, and so forth. In fact, it is even legal to repackage government documents and sell them—if, that is, you can find a buyer for documents that are freely and easily available elsewhere. The rationale behind this rule is that since works created by government employees in the course of their work have been entirely created and published under public subsidy, members of the public should own those works and be able to do with them as they see fit. (A somewhat similar argument about the published products of publicly funded research will be discussed in Chapter 12 on open access.)

When it comes to copyright and government documents, however, there are two very important distinctions to be made. The first is the distinction between works created by a government employee *as a part of his or her official duties*, and works created by a government employee in the course of some other endeavor. To illustrate this difference: Suppose that an employee working in the Department of Education spends his morning composing a memorandum concerning educational policy that will be published on the Department's website later that month. Then, while on his lunch break (and in his role as a private citizen), that same employee writes a letter to the editor of the local newspaper about the performance of the local school board. In this scenario, the memorandum that he spent the morning writing would be a government document (because it was written in the discharge of his official job duties), and therefore neither he nor anyone else would hold copyright in that work. However, the letter he wrote while on his lunch break (which was not written in the course of his official duties nor in his official capacity as a Department of Education employee) would not be a government document, and he would hold the copyright in that work.

The second important distinction to be made is that between *government* employees and *public* employees— and this distinction is particularly important in the context of scholarly communication, because a large number of academic scholars and researchers work for public colleges and universities, and are therefore both authors and public employees. Furthermore, the scope of their jobs is often quite broad, and the works that they produce as scholars very often arguably fall within the scope of their "official duties." For example, a faculty member who writes a syllabus for her class is quite clearly creating that syllabus as part of her official duties as an academic instructor. If she then writes a letter to the editor of a journal in her academic field (even if she does so on her lunch break), this also may arguably fall within her official duties, since there is for most faculty members a formal expectation that they will contribute to the professional and academic conversation in their fields. And, of course, it is a basic job expectation for most faculty members to publish professional and academic articles and books, which are generally written (substantially, at least) on "work time" and are most certainly produced as a part of their official duties.

This reality raises two important questions: First, does this mean that an academic's publications constitute "works for hire" under copyright law, and second, if the faculty member is employed at a public institution, does that mean that the academic's work is a government document?

The answer to the first question is usually no (see below for a more detailed discussion). The answer to the second question is almost invariably no, because the public sector and the government sector are not the same thing; the latter is a subset of the former. This distinction may sometimes be a bit confusing, but when it comes to copyright law, it is very important. Without going into too much tiresome detail, it is probably sufficient to note that (in the United States, at least) the faculty of public institutions of higher education are public employees, but not government ones. The rules that govern the copyright status of their academic work are set at the institutional level, and are usually the same as those that govern the copyright status of academic work by faculty members at private institutions.

How does U.K. copyright law apply to documents created wholly or partially on the public dime?

In the United Kingdom and other Commonwealth realms, there is a set of special copyright rules known as Crown copyright. These rules apply to documents created by the government and its employees, and they vary somewhat from realm to realm. In the United Kingdom, the history of Crown copyright is complex and its application today can be confusing, but the basic thing to understand is that whereas U.S. government documents are usually ineligible for copyright protection, in the United Kingdom the copyright in such documents is generally held by the monarch.[6] There are exceptions, and it is also worth noting that the U.K. government often releases Crown copyright works to the public under an Open Government Licence. However, this does not change the fact that the copyright itself remains with the monarch.

How does copyright work?

Copyright law (as embodied in Title 17 of the U.S. Code and in the Copyright, Designs and Patents Act of 1988 in the United Kingdom) is complex in many ways and does many different things, but for our purposes its most important features can be boiled down to a reasonably simple summary: If you create an original work of authorship and express it in a fixed medium (by writing it down on paper or on a computer, or by recording it in some other more or less permanent way), the law grants you a set of exclusive but limited rights with regard to that work. Among others, these usually include the exclusive rights to copy and distribute the work (for example, by publishing it), to perform or transmit it, and to create derivative works from it.

Your rights as a copyright holder are *exclusive* in that they are yours alone until you elect to grant them to someone else, and they are *limited* in that they are not absolute and do not last forever—after a certain period of time, copyrighted works pass into the public domain and are no longer subject to copyright restrictions. In other words, although you have the exclusive right to copy and distribute an original article that you have written, others may copy and distribute it in limited ways that are characterized in the law as "fair use" (in the United States) or "fair dealing" (in the United Kingdom). (For convenience, I will refer to this concept simply as "fair use" from now on.) The particulars of fair use can be somewhat blurry and are sometimes contested in court, but the basic concept behind them is well established: Your exclusive rights as a copyright holder have limits, and the public has the legal right to do certain things with your original work that may appear to infringe to some degree on the exclusivity of your rights. More on this topic below.

It is worth noting that in both the United States and the United Kingdom, you do not have to register your work in any formal way in order to hold copyright in it. Formal copyright registration is available if you want it, but as soon as you have written down your idea or otherwise recorded it in a fixed medium, you immediately hold the copyright in that recorded expression of the idea. But it's also very important to note that ideas themselves cannot be copyrighted. This has serious implications for scholarly communication. It means, for example, that if you discover a new chemical element and write an article about your discovery, no one has the right to publish that article without your permission. However, anyone who learns about your discovery of the new chemical element is free to write her own account of the discovery and to publish that account, as long as what she is publishing is her own original expression of the idea. It is the *documented expression* of an idea, not the idea itself, that is copyrightable.

As briefly mentioned above, one feature of your rights as a copyright holder is the fact that you can transfer your copyright (in whole or in part) to someone else. When scholars submit their work for publication as journal articles or monographs, they very often transfer copyright to the publisher as a condition of publication. And some publishers (and institutions and funding agencies) also require authors to grant to the public a license that transfers to the public some or all of the prerogatives that the law provides to copyright holders. We will discuss both of these issues in a little more depth later in this chapter.

What is fair use and how does it work?

Fair use is one of those legal topics that can lead to endless argument and hypothetical speculation, but the basic principles are relatively simple: The rights of a copyright holder are exclusive, but not absolute—they are limited. This means that, for example, while the law grants the copyright holder *exclusive* control over the copying and distribution of his work, it does not give him *complete* control over those uses. There are enshrined in both American and British law types of use that technically fall within the copyright holder's exclusive prerogatives, but that are nevertheless permitted to the general public. These exceptions provide balance between protecting the interests of those who created the work and those of the general public who stand to benefit from using it.

The reason that fair use can lead to endless argument is that its parameters are necessarily somewhat fuzzy. Here is how fair use is defined in U.S. copyright law:

> Notwithstanding the provisions of sections 106 and 106A, the fair use of a copyrighted work, including such use by reproduction in copies or phonorecords or by any other means specified by that section, for purposes such as criticism, comment, news reporting, teaching (including multiple copies for classroom use), scholarship, or research, is not an infringement of copyright. In determining whether the use made of a work in any particular case is a fair use the factors to be considered shall include—

> (1) the purpose and character of the use, including whether such use is of a commercial nature or is for nonprofit educational purposes;
> (2) the nature of the copyrighted work;

(3) the amount and substantiality of the portion used in relation to the copyrighted work as a whole; and

(4) the effect of the use upon the potential market for or value of the copyrighted work.
The fact that a work is unpublished shall not itself bar a finding of fair use if such finding is made upon consideration of all the above factors.[7]

It is significant that this section of the law does not say "Here is a list of uses that the courts will always consider to be fair." Instead, it presents a list of variables that should be considered when contemplating a particular use. They lead us to ask ourselves questions like "How much of the copyrighted work am I considering copying?" and "Am I planning to use the copy or copies for commercial purposes?" The answer to any of these individual questions will not usually give us a completely clear-cut indication of whether our proposed use is fair, but taken together they will help us figure out how much legal risk we are assuming by undertaking the proposed use. In some cases, it will be clear that the risk is minimal; in some cases, it will be larger.

It should also be noted that none of these four tests constitutes a legal trump card—a proposed use may completely "fail" one of these tests and still be fair. A classic example of how this might work is the "home taping" scenario: You own a legitimate copy of a music album on LP or CD, but you only have a cassette tape player in your car. You record the entirety of the album onto a cassette tape so that you can listen to it while driving. This use would arguably fail test #3 (amount and substantiality) because you are copying the entire copyrighted work. However, if you own a legally obtained copy of the work, your sole purpose in making the copy is for personal convenience, and you do not plan to give or sell the copy to someone else so that he will not have to buy a copy of the album from the copyright holder, then this proposed use may pass all the other tests so well that it can still be reasonably construed as fair.

Fair use evaluations are up to the individuals who are contemplating making use of copyrighted works. Importantly, fair use evaluations are not up to the copyright holder—one does not ask the copyright holder whether a proposed use is fair. A copyright holder may completely disagree with you that your proposed use is fair, but that disagreement is legally irrelevant: It is the law, not the copyright holder, that defines the rights and privileges of both copyright holders and the general public.

In U.K. law, the concept of "fair dealing" is roughly analogous to that of fair use in the United States, though its parameters are somewhat more restrictive than those of fair use—and it should be noted that the term "fair dealing" has a different meaning in U.S. law than it does in U.K. law.

How long does copyright last?

One very important limitation on copyright is its term. In the United States, all copyrighted works will eventually enter the public domain. How long an author (or her assigns) may retain copyright in her work will vary quite a bit according to several factors.

In the United States, anything that was published prior to 1923 is now in the public domain. (The laws in effect at that time provided for an initial copyright term of twenty-eight years, which could be extended for another twenty-eight before the work entered the public domain.) The great majority of works published before 1964 are also now in the public domain, because the laws in effect at that time provided for renewal but very few copyright holders took advantage of it before the end of the twenty-eight-year copyright period.

However, the law changed in 1992 and then again in 1998. For works copyrighted between 1964 and 1977, a second term of copyright is now granted automatically, and the second term is twenty years longer. Thus, the copyright period for a work copyrighted between 1964 and 1977 is now ninety-five years, and no registration or renewal is required.[8]

Who holds the copyright in the work of scholars that are employed by academic institutions?

This a very interesting question in the context of scholarly communication, because in most employment situations, the writing or other creative work that one does in one's capacity as an employee remains the property of the employer. If, for example, you work for an auto-parts manufacturer and are assigned to write a procedural handbook for new employees in your division, that handbook will typically be considered a "work for hire" under copyright law and, even though it is your original work, the copyright will be held by the company you work for. (In most cases, this arrangement should be spelled out explicitly in the employment contract you sign at the time of hire.) The same goes for corporate memos, proposals, internal research reports, and other kinds of writing or creative work that one generates as a part of one's job duties.

In this regard, academia is somewhat unusual. In the academic context, faculty members are generally expected to produce copyrightable written documents (scholarly articles, books, etc.), and if those faculty members are on the tenure track, such production is quite explicitly a condition of continued employment: If you do not publish you will not get tenure and will lose your job. Despite the fact that scholarly writings of various kinds might look very much like "works for hire," copyright in the original work of faculty members usually remains with the author, even though it is typically created on work time and using institutional resources.

The policy landscape is complex, however. For example, as of this writing Columbia University does not claim copyright in "books, monographs, articles, and similar works" that are produced by individual faculty members, but it does claim copyright in materials that the University itself formally publishes (such as "journals, periodicals, yearbooks, compendia, anthologies and films published by divisions of the University") and in "some works produced as a collaborative effort under the aegis of a school or department"—though not in all of them.[9] When online courses are developed by faculty members, copyright questions can become more complex, and different institutions deal with them in different ways. It is also worth noting that there are many manifestations of intellectual property other than scholarly writings and courses, and in academia these may include patents that are granted in products and processes developed on campus. It is very common for academic and research institutions to claim ownership of such patents.

The bottom line, for faculty members as for all other employees, is the importance of reading very carefully the terms of employment before accepting an academic job. Regardless of what intellectual-property rights are granted to authors by law, employers generally have the right to require the abdication of some or all of those rights as a condition of employment. (If that sounds strange or unreasonable, consider the fact that although I have the legal right to speak my mind freely, I also have the right to enter into a contract with my employer that requires me to keep certain information confidential. Similarly, although the law grants me the copyright in my original work as an author, the law also allows me to enter into a contract that requires me to assign copyright to my employer.)

What is the difference between copyright protection and patent protection?

Both copyright law and patent law give certain exclusive rights to the original creators of intellectual products. However, these two kinds of protection apply to very different kinds of intellectual property: Copyright applies to works of authorship—expressions of creative or interpretive ideas that have been fixed in some kind of format (a written document, a musical score, an original film, a sound recording, etc.), whereas patent law applies to original inventions (machines, production processes, chemical compositions, etc.).

The particular sets of exclusive rights that copyright and patents grant to their holders are different. As discussed above, the exclusive rights owned by a copyright holder have to do with the exploitation of a particular recorded expression of an idea: Thus, if I hold the copyright in a biography of Abraham Lincoln, I hold the exclusive right to publish that book, to copy it, to create derivative works based upon it, and so forth. I do not hold the copyright in any of the *component facts* of the book—for example, I cannot copyright the fact that Abraham Lincoln was born in Kentucky in 1861, or that he worked as an attorney before beginning his career in politics. But my written discussion of those facts is subject to copyright as long as it involves some degree of original thought and explication.

A patent represents a rather different type of intellectual property. It grants the patent holder exclusive control over an invention, allowing him to stop others from producing or selling products based on that invention for a limited period of time. The invention may be a physical machine of some kind, or it might be a production process, an original chemical compound, or some other invention that is conceptual or process-based rather than a concrete object. Like copyright law, patent law varies from country to country.

Another important area of intellectual property law applies to trademarks, but discussion of these is outside the scope of this book.

Are there international copyright and patent laws?

The short answer to this question is no—intellectual property law varies significantly from country to country, and this causes quite a bit of trouble, particularly given the global reach of the Internet. But that answer is incomplete, because while there is no statutory international copyright law, there are binding international treaties that govern the disposition and protection of intellectual property, including copyright. The World Intellectual Property Organization (WIPO) was created in 1967 as a specialized agency of the United Nations, with a charge to "promote the protection of intellectual property throughout the world through cooperation among States."[10] As of this writing, 189 states are members of WIPO, and the organization administers 26 international treaties.[11] While these treaties are important and do have at least some effect on international behavior, it should be noted that they are binding only on those nations that choose to enter into them—and that even among those, observance of the treaty terms is far from universally consistent. (Of course, the same can be said of compliance with statutory copyright law within nations.)

That last note is worth emphasizing. When it comes to intellectual property protections on the international stage, there are two important variables: differences in the terms of intellectual property law between countries, and differences in the cultural norms regarding respect for intellectual property. Not all nations, even signatories to the various WIPO treaties, take equally seriously the restrictions imposed by either those treaties or their own internal laws, and not all groups of people within a particular nation are equally scrupulous about observing copyright law. The inconsistency of copyright restrictions from country to country, and widely differing cultural attitudes toward copyright and intellectual property rights generally across countries and regions, contribute to a rather muddled international situation. This muddle is only made deeper by the Internet, which makes so much intellectual property easily available to billions around the world at the click of a mouse. On college campuses with international student bodies, it can be difficult to explain to students from faraway countries with very different cultural understandings of intellectual property why, for example, it may not be acceptable to download five years' worth of content from a particular journal, upload it to a cloud-based storage facility, and make it available to one's friends and colleagues back home.

Why do authors assign their copyright to publishers?

Scholarly authors are different from novelists, freelance journalists, and other kinds of writers in many ways, one of the most important of which is that they do not typically expect to make money directly from sales of their work. Producing scholarship is one of the requirements of the job they do every day, for which they are paid a salary. In other words, in most cases they have already been paid for their writing. They typically publish it not in order to get paid again, but for the purposes of publicly certifying its quality, demonstrating that they are the originators of the ideas or discoveries in question, furthering their scholarly disciplines, and keeping their jobs. Not only are scholarly authors almost never paid for the articles they contribute to academic and scientific journals, but in fact, they give something up in return for the privilege of being published in those outlets: They typically give away their copyrights in the work, handing over to the publisher all of the exclusive rights that the law granted them when the work was produced.

It may seem strange that scholarly authors would be willing to do this, especially if they are providing content at no charge to a journal publisher who will turn around and sell access to it—in some cases, at very high prices. Why would an author simply give away to a commercial publisher the ability to make money on his original work?

In fact, although this situation might look like a give-away, it is in fact a quid pro quo exchange: The author trades rights for services. What the author hands over to the publisher is copyright (or, in some cases, a more limited publication right), and what the author receives in exchange are editorial and peer-review services, certification of quality, formal distribution, archiving, and other services that authors tend to value quite highly. As we discussed in Chapter 2, scholarly authors care very much where and how their articles and books are published, and for most scholarly and scientific authors giving up copyright may feel like a small price to pay for a career-enhancing (and potentially career-making) publication with a prestigious journal or book publisher. The fact that the author would not have had any reasonable expectation of making money from publication of the article in the first place makes the decision that much easier. (There are more tradeoffs involved than these, however, some of which will be discussed in the chapter dealing with open access.)

For books in particular, the calculus of this decision making can be a bit more complicated. While authors of articles in scholarly journals are almost never paid, book authors do often receive royalties from sales of their books, and this can factor into the publication choices the authors of monographs make. However, in this situation there are also other tradeoffs to consider: For tenure-seeking scholars, getting a book published with a trade press like Basic Books or Little, Brown (which market their publications to a general readership) might not carry the same prestige as publishing it with a major university press (which signals to tenure committees a greater level of academic seriousness). The royalties may be greater when you publish with a trade press, but the long-term professional cost can be high if doing so makes you seem like a less serious scholar. In either case, however, the author generally assigns copyright to the publisher regardless.

What are "orphan works"?

The term "orphan work" is commonly used to refer to works that are known still to be under copyright, but for which the copyright holder is unknown. For example, if a book was written in 1780, its copyright status is uncontroversial: Because it was written so long ago, we can be confident that it is no longer under copyright protection in any known jurisdiction. That book is now in the public domain. If a book was written in 1930, however, it may or may not still be under copyright; different legal jurisdictions grant different terms of copyright and place different renewal requirements on copyright holders. If a book was written in 1990 in the United States, it is surely still under copyright. However, if the author is unknown, or if the author's name is known but she cannot be found, or if the author has died and it is not clear whether or not her copyright passed to an heir or assign, then this book may be referred to as an "orphan work."

Orphan works present a particularly difficult problem in scholarly communication because in many cases there may be no legal impediment to copying and redistributing them as widely and freely as possible, but it is not possible to determine for certain whether such impediments exist.

There are several strategies available for dealing with orphan works. The easiest is simply to proceed on the assumption that the work has passed into the public domain, or at least that the copyright holder (if alive) will not object to her work being treated that way. One might then copy and redistribute the work freely, waiting to be contacted by the rights holder in the event of any objection. One problem with this approach is that it is technically illegal, even if its real-world impact on another's rights is likely to be minimal. Another problem is that it assumes the rights holder will find out about the illegal use and thus be able to object to it if so inclined; that is a fairly big assumption. And, of course, the third problem is that if the rights holder does get wind of the infringing use, she could theoretically sue the infringer—though in the case of orphan works, that risk will usually be quite low.

Another strategy is simply to play it safe, and treat the orphan work as if its owner is someone who has declined to provide reuse permission. In this case, one would limit oneself to making use of the work in ways consistent with fair use. The upside of this strategy is that it can easily be defended both ethically and legally; the downside is that it may involve a greater-than-necessary level of restriction on the sharing of the content.

A third strategy, one that treads a middle ground between these two, is to use the work as if it were freely available but attach to it an affirmative public statement expressing one's desire to identify and locate the rights holder and one's willingness to comply with any takedown notice that might be forthcoming should the rights holder make herself known. One can often see evidence of this approach online, where the owner of a website might post photographs or sound files alongside a notice saying something like "I believe that this work is in the public domain; however, if you are the copyright holder and would like me to take it down, please contact me." Perhaps the most notable example of this strategy was that attempted by HathiTrust in its Orphan Works Project; for further discussion of this project, see Chapter 8.

What is the difference between copyright infringement and plagiarism?

Plagiarism and copyright infringement are related to each other in that each involves the appropriation of someone else's work. However, the differences between them are very important. For one thing, one can plagiarize without committing a copyright infringement, and one can infringe copyright without plagiarizing. Another important distinction is that copyright infringement is illegal, while plagiarism is not.

Plagiarism consists in presenting someone else's work as your own. It might be done in a wholesale manner (by, for example, finding an eighteenth-century book manuscript written by someone else and publishing it under your own name as if you were the author) or in smaller and more subtle ways (by, for example, incorporating a few sentences of someone else's work into an original work of your own without attributing that material to its author).

In neither case have you infringed copyright, because an eighteenth-century book manuscript will be in the public domain and copying and redistributing a few sentences of someone else's text will generally be considered fair use under copyright law, whether you do it with or without attribution. But in both cases you have taken someone else's intellectual work and presented it to the world as if it were your own, and that is plagiarism.

Copyright infringement, on the other hand, means treating a work in which someone else holds the copyright as if you were the copyright holder. So, for example, if you found a book manuscript written in 2005 and published it without the author's permission, this would almost certainly constitute copyright infringement even if you acknowledge the writer's authorship. Similarly, if you take an article from a recent journal and distribute copies of it to the 3,000 members of an e-mail listserv or post it online for others to download, you will almost certainly be in breach of copyright (unless the article has been licensed for this kind of distribution and reuse—more discussion of this topic below). In neither case have you pretended to be the author, which would be plagiarism, but in both cases you have infringed on the copyright holder's exclusive rights.

Of course, it's possible to plagiarize and infringe copyright simultaneously. If you were to steal your friend's book manuscript and publish it as your own work, you would be both plagiarizing (by presenting his work as your own) and infringing on his copyright (by publishing his work without permission). So plagiarism and copyright infringement are related in some important ways and can sometimes happen simultaneously, but they are separate issues and the differences between them are very important to understand.

The legal difference also matters quite a bit. While plagiarism may be considered a "crime" of scholarship, there is no law against it—it is a breach of professional and academic ethics only. Copyright infringement, however, is not only illegal, but in particularly severe cases may be considered a criminal (as distinct from civil) offense and may be punishable by imprisonment. To rise to this level, however, the infringement would need to have caused serious and demonstrable harm.

What is the "copyleft" movement, and what are its implications for scholarly communication?

The "copyleft" movement—a not particularly subtle pun on the word "copyright"—has its origins in the free software movement, especially the work of programmer and activist Richard Stallman. (Stallman insists on the term "free" software rather than "open" or "open source," for reasons he outlines on his website.[12]) As Stallman explains it, "copyleft is a general method for making a program (or other work) free, and requiring all modified and extended versions of the program to be free as well."[13] While copyleft is most often considered in the context of software, the principles that underlie it have interesting implications for other kinds of intellectual property as well.

In the context of scholarly communication, the copyleft movement is perhaps most notable for having given birth to the Creative Commons licensing initiative, which is the subject of our next question.

What are Creative Commons licenses and how do they interact with copyright?

Creative Commons was established in 2001 to enable "the sharing and use of creativity and knowledge through free legal tools," the most notable of which is a suite of Creative

Commons (CC) copyright licenses.[14] These licenses give copyright holders a way of signaling that they grant to the public some or all of the prerogatives that would otherwise be theirs alone under copyright law. Different CC licenses grant to the public more or fewer of those prerogatives. Thus, for example, if an author makes her work publicly available under a CC-BY-NC-ND license, that means that anyone who wishes to is free to copy and redistribute the work as long as he credits her as the original author (hence the BY, or "attribution" element) and does so for noncommercial (NC) purposes. This license also restricts the creation of derivative works (ND) without the author's permission.

The most liberal of the CC licenses is CC BY, which basically grants to the public all of the prerogatives that copyright holders have under the law. Under a CC BY license, anyone may copy, redistribute, and create derivative works from the copyrighted material, as long as the author is given attribution as the creator of the original work. Authors who license their work under CC BY are still technically the copyright holders; however, for all *functional* purposes they have placed the work into the public domain, since members of the general public now have the right to do whatever they wish with it just as if it were not under copyright. (The only difference is that a CC BY license does impose on those who reuse the work a contractual obligation to acknowledge the work's original authorship—and, of course, the author may revoke the CC license at some point in the future if he wishes.)

CC has also created a tool by which an author may signal that he has placed his work officially into the public domain, thus taking it out of the realm of copyright control altogether. This tool is not technically a license; it is, rather, a waiver of copyright and is represented by the symbol CC0.

Are Creative Commons licenses related to access licenses?

In the scholarly publishing world, the term "license" is used in a slightly different sense as well, one that reflects a different kind of interaction with copyright and copyright law.

During the print era, libraries brokered access to expensive scholarly and scientific content on behalf of their patrons by engaging in a relatively straightforward practice: buying physical documents, organizing them to make them findable by students and scholars, and preserving them against loss or disintegration. This practice was not necessarily easy, but in a legal and market sense it was pretty simple. The well-established legal doctrine known as First Sale made it clear that once a library or an individual had obtained a legitimate copy of a copyrighted document, that physical copy could be shared freely—as long as the sharing behavior did not infringe on the copyright holder's exclusive rights. So, for example, if you own a copy of a novel, the First Sale doctrine says that you can lend that copy or give it away or sell it to someone else—or, for that matter, burn it, throw it in the trash, cut it up and turn it into an art project, or tear it in half and give half of it to your neighbor. All of these are legal and legitimate uses of your physical copy of the intellectual work.

What you may *not* do (beyond the bounds of fair use) is create copies of the work, create derivative versions of its content, publicly perform it, and so forth. Such uses would go beyond manipulation or disposition of the physical object that you own, and get into the realm of something that you do not own—the content of the book itself. This distinction—that between the physical copy of the book and the intellectual content of the book—is an essential one that goes to the heart of copyright law.

Unfortunately, that essential distinction becomes strangely fuzzy in the virtual world of online information—

a world in which, when we talk about ownership of documents, the terms "ownership" and "document" should really both be placed in scare quotes. After all, when you buy an e-book, what does it mean to "own" a "copy" of it? It might mean that a copy of the book has been downloaded as a text file to your tablet computer or reader device. This is the scenario under which e-book ownership most closely resembles ownership of a physical book—you really do own a "copy" of the work, and you have direct control over that copy.

But what if your e-book does not live within the memory of your personal computer or reader device, but is instead hosted on the Internet? In this case, it makes less sense to say that you have purchased a copy of the book, and more sense to say that you have purchased a right of access. In return for the purchase price, the owner and host of the book gives you a more or less permanent right to read a copy of the book that lives elsewhere—almost as if you went to a bookstore, paid for a book, and instead of taking the book home were given a permanent right to read the book through the store's window. (That might not sound like a great arrangement unless you consider that when it comes to e-books, an agreement like this allows you to carry access to hundreds or thousands of books with you wherever you go, as long as you have Internet access.)

In the world of pleasure reading, online-only access can work fairly well, particularly with the growing affordability and popularity of e-book reading devices. In an academic context, however, online access is not generally considered acceptable without the ability to download. Scholars and scientists often need to be able to file away articles for future reference, and need to have access to those documents at times and in places where the Internet may not be available. So academic libraries typically negotiate with publishers not just for read-only, online access to documents, but for the ability to download and store them as well, and they negotiate these rights on an institutional basis so that everyone affiliated with the institution will be able to make use of the documents in question.

However, a system whereby a community of thousands (or even tens of thousands) of people have an effectively unlimited ability to download, copy, and redistribute copyrighted content is one that tends to raise concerns for copyright holders. For this reason, the terms that govern institutional access to online content are laid out in licenses, the terms of which are negotiated between the copyright holder and the purchasing institution.

Licenses are contracts, and like all contracts, they lay out both rights and obligations for each party. A typical access license will, for example, put the publisher under obligation to provide the content that has been paid for, and to rectify access problems (such as server malfunction or authentication failures) in a timely way. It might also lay out the ways in which the publisher will provide for permanent ongoing access in the event that the publisher goes out of business (by archiving the content with a third-party provider, for example). The same license will enjoin the library to take concrete steps to ensure that unauthorized users do not gain access to the licensed content, and to pay each annual invoice promptly.

Do license terms override legal rights such as fair use?

The short answer is "yes," but a more accurate answer would be more complicated than that. It is in the very nature of contracts that they limit the rights of the parties beyond the limitations imposed by law. In other words, a contract is the mechanism by which two parties agree to do things that the law does not require them to do, or to refrain from doing things that the law allows them to do. So, for example, no matter where you live, the law probably allows you to wear any color shirt you wish. But if you enter into a valid employment contract that requires you to wear a purple shirt while on the job, that requirement has legal force. Similarly, the law will allow you to enter into a contract that includes a nondisclosure agreement (enjoining you from speaking to others about the terms of the contract), despite whatever free speech rights the law may otherwise provide. In both cases, these terms have legal force not because there are laws that say "you must wear a purple shirt" or "you may not speak freely," but rather because there are laws that say "you must abide by the terms of valid contracts." (Of course, if the contract is not valid, then its terms are not binding. Making sure that contracts are valid before they are signed is one of the things for which lawyers get paid a lot of money.)

This principle applies when it comes to access licenses and fair use as well. Although the law allows you to share copies of a copyrighted document within the bounds of fair use, you may nevertheless enter into a valid contract that restricts you from sharing copies at all. As long as the contract itself meets the standards of legal validity, its terms will be binding on you, and those terms will inevitably be more restrictive than the law itself—again, this is the whole purpose of contracts.

All of that being said, the tension between license terms and broader legal rights is one of which librarians tend to be keenly aware, and when negotiating the terms of access licenses on behalf of their campus communities they will very often work to incorporate language that explicitly recognizes fair use rights and incorporates those rights into the allowances made for patrons by the license.

Why do we call copyright infringers "pirates"?

The practice of referring to copyright infringement, especially egregious or large-scale acts, as "piracy" and infringers as "pirates" has a long history, one that actually predates the establishment of modern copyright law— known instances of this usage go back as far as 1603.[15] Since pirates were known for their practice of stealing the property of others, it became common to refer to those who infringe on copyright holders' exclusive rights by the same term.

With the rise of the Internet in the late twentieth century, and the concomitant dramatic rise in the ease and frequency of copyright infringement, the term began to arise more often, particularly in the context of music. In 1999 an online music service called Napster was founded to facilitate what came to be called "peer-to-peer file sharing"— or, in other words, the uploading of files to the Internet for mass duplication and download. Napster made it not only possible but also easy for people to create digital copies of sound recordings, put those copies online, and in turn download copies of music that other people had made. Since the source files used in this practice were, for the most part, copyrighted songs, the widespread use of Napster constituted copyright piracy on a massive scale. For the next few years debate raged as to the ethics of file "sharing" and its impact (if any) on the fortunes of musicians and record labels. Napster was eventually sued, successfully, by the Recording Industry of America and was shut down in 2001.[16] The Napster name was later sold and used as a trademark for a commercial online music service.

The concept of piracy has a more vexed history in the context of scholarly communication. We will close this chapter by examining some of that recent history, specifically the case of Sci-Hub.

What is Sci-Hub and why is it so controversial?

Sci-Hub is the brainchild of Alexandra Elbakyan, as of this writing a graduate student at the National Research University in Russia (according to her LinkedIn page[17]). She has also studied at Georgia Tech and at Albert-Ludwigs University. As a student she grew frustrated with her limited access to legitimately licensed scholarly and scientific content, and so she hacked her way past the access protocols to a number of journals and downloaded the articles she needed. According to one of many online profiles written about her, she then found that her fellow students wanted access to those articles as well, so she created a website on which to make them freely available.[18] Eventually her site joined forces with a similar service called LibGen, and its content was expanded by the collection of anonymously donated (and some allegedly stolen) campus network passwords. Sci-Hub reportedly now contains over 50 million articles, the vast majority of them from subscription journals, all made available to the public for free.

The controversy over Sci-Hub is, unsurprisingly, both great and multidimensional. The most obvious controversy has to do with copyright. No one disputes that Sci-Hub represents one of the most massive examples of systematic copyright infringement in history, and there is little question that Sci-Hub's activity is illegal. (Elbakyan herself was successfully sued by one large scientific publisher, resulting in a temporary shutdown of her site, and is currently under indictment and believed to be in hiding in Russia.[19]) But whether her behavior represents an unethical breach of copyright or a praiseworthy act of defiance against the indefensible exploitation of scholarly and scientific knowledge (or something ethically in between) is a topic of intense debate within the scholarly and scientific community.

Another controversy has to do with the ethics of acquiring and sharing access credentials. Sci-Hub copies published papers not only by hacking past access restrictions, but also by gathering usernames and passwords from academics whose campuses have licensed access to the publications in question. Some have accused Sci-Hub of using deceptive "phishing" emails in order to elicit that information from academics, a charge that Elbakyan has been very careful not to exactly deny.[20] Whether Sci-Hub gathers network credentials by deception or not, the practice of doing so raises very serious ethical and security issues. By sharing their network credentials with unauthorized people or organizations (whatever their intentions or motivations), students and faculty open themselves up not only to institutional sanction but also to potential identity theft. On many campuses, the login credentials used to access licensed information resources are also used to access e-mail accounts, personnel records, tax forms, patient data, and other highly sensitive information.

But there is a larger question at issue here, and it is perhaps the most controversial of all: Is it morally acceptable that scholarly and scientific publications be made available only to those who are able and willing to pay for them, or who are served by third-party access brokers like libraries? This is not so much a question about how scholarly communication works as it is a question about social justice in the context of scholarly communication. For more discussion of this issue, see Chapter 12.

6

WHAT IS THE ROLE
OF THE LIBRARY?

What do we mean when we say "libraries"?

Obviously, there are many different kinds of libraries with a variety of missions: Public libraries, corporate libraries, hospital libraries, subscription libraries, school libraries, and academic libraries all exist to do subtly but significantly different things. Since this book deals specifically with scholarly communication, though, we will use the word "libraries" to refer to academic libraries at institutions of higher education.

*What is the difference between an academic library
and a research library?*

Having agreed to limit our examination to academic libraries, however, we are still left with the important differences between, on the one hand, libraries at community colleges, liberal arts colleges, and comprehensive universities (all of which tend to be charged mainly with supporting campus teaching and learning) and, on the other hand, those at research-intensive universities and institutes (which are charged with supporting extensive advanced research programs in addition to classroom instruction and undergraduate study). For readers who have heard the terms "academic library" and "research library" used more or less interchangeably and may have wondered whether there is a difference, the answer is yes—virtually all research libraries are academic libraries, but a great many academic libraries are not research libraries. This too, however, is a distinction that we will largely fudge in this book: For our purposes here, the word "library" can usefully refer to academic libraries across the spectrum of instructional and research-focused institutions. At points in the discussion where the distinction between those kinds of institutions becomes important, we will deal with it explicitly.

Why do we have libraries? What do they do?

Libraries are established and supported by their host institutions to perform a variety of functions. Three of the most important of these are *brokerage*, *access*, and *curation*.

Brokerage is the function by which the library pools money on behalf of its host community (faculty, students, staff) and uses that money to buy a bigger and higher-quality collection of information resources than individual members of the community would be able to afford on their own. Most obviously these resources include printed books and other physical documents, electronic books and journals, online databases, and other information products, but libraries offer space in which to work, research services of various kinds, and equipment and software as well. Brokerage has always been one of the centrally important roles of a library. No student or faculty member could possibly hope to pay on her own for access to all of the information resources she needs in order to do her scholarly work, so the library procures that access on her behalf and that of the rest of the faculty and student body. Historically, the upside of this arrangement has been that the campus community gets access to a very large collection of scholarly content; the downside is that since all members of the community share that access with each other, there is some inconvenience involved—especially with regard to physical documents, which have to be housed centrally and can only be used by one person at a time. (In most cases, online documents can be used by multiple people at once—and, of course, remotely.)

Access to content, for the whole community, is the purpose of brokerage. By paying on behalf of the campus community, the library enables all within it to have access to the purchased or licensed content. But the library's role in ensuring access goes beyond negotiating license terms and paying for access; it also includes making sure that the physical documents are organized in such a way that they can be found, and overseeing the ongoing availability of the online documents to which access has been licensed. Both of these access functions involve ongoing (and sometimes very staff-intensive) work on the library's part, some of which will be discussed in more detail later in this chapter.

Curation has to do with the ongoing care and protection of documents to ensure their future availability to the community that the library serves. Libraries curate books and other physical documents by monitoring their condition and either replacing or repairing them as needed—and they curate the physical collection as a whole by both adding materials to it and withdrawing materials from it when space requires, or when those materials are superseded by better versions. Libraries curate online access to locally digitized collections (about which more below) by maintaining format standards, providing server space, and storing them robustly. They curate licensed access to online documents by monitoring their ongoing availability, ensuring that contracts are negotiated well and paid promptly, and responding quickly when access is interrupted for some reason.

Do libraries provide a free service to their patrons?

This is actually one of the more pernicious myths about library services: the proposition that they are provided for free. This myth is sometimes propounded by librarians themselves in a sincere but misguided attempt to convince more people to avail themselves of library services, and sometimes by library supporters in a sincere but misguided attempt to act as boosters and cheerleaders for libraries.

In reality, of course, no library does anything for free. Library patrons are most assuredly paying for the services they receive—but since the payments are made indirectly (usually in the form of property taxes, tuition, or student fees) and since payment is separated in both time and space from the experience of library services, those services can easily give the false impression of being offered at no charge. In other words, the fact that you can walk into a library, select five books, and take them home with you without any money changing hands during the transaction makes the transaction feel as if it came without cost. In reality, however, the money changed hands earlier, and made its way indirectly from your pocket to the library's budget.

Why is this a point worth making? Because the proposition that libraries offer "free services" poses two risks that are mirror images of each other. First, it poses the risk that library services will be undervalued by those whose financial support is essential to their survival. It is a common rule of thumb in economics that we tend to value least those things in which we have the least invested, and for this reason alone it is unwise for any library to pretend that its patrons have not made concrete monetary investments in the library and its services.

More subtly, the claim that libraries provide "free services" is risky because it simply does not pass the smell test. Anyone who hears that claim and takes even a few moments to consider it will immediately recognize its falsity and may then start to wonder whether other things said by librarians (and their supporters) are actually trustworthy.

For libraries and their boosters who want to encourage better and more widespread use of the library, a more accurate and effective message might be: "Come see how we are making wise and effective use of the money you have entrusted us with."   ·

How do libraries build and manage their collections?

Historically, one of the centrally important duties of librarianship has been the selection of books and journals for the collection, and the subsequent management of that collection—a process that includes both selection and withdrawal of materials as curricular and research needs change and as budgets and available space require. For as long as academic libraries have existed, the subdiscipline of librarianship known as collection development has been one of the foundational elements of the profession.

Of course, when it has come to deciding which books and journals will be part of the collections, librarians have not historically operated in a vacuum. They call on faculty and students to provide input, and at some academic institutions it is actually the faculty themselves who select books for the library collection, using budgets allocated to them for that purpose by the library. (This model is much more common in smaller liberal arts colleges than in larger comprehensive or research universities.)

Traditionally, library collection development has focused on three basic strategic tools: the *firm order*, the *approval plan,* and the *subscription.* We shall examine each of these in turn.

The *firm order* is the most basic building block of library collection development. The term refers to the simple ordering of a book, whether it be selected by a librarian or suggested for purchase by a patron. In response to the felt need for a particular book, the library contacts the publisher or a third-party vendor and places an order for it. This is called a "firm order" because it represents the library's definite intention to acquire the book and place it permanently in the collection.

Approval plans work very differently. An approval plan is an arrangement whereby the library works with a third-party book vendor (or "jobber") to create a detailed profile of the library's collecting priorities. The profile will identify publishers and subject areas in which the library has a particular interest, as well as those in which the library has no interest. It will further identify what are sometimes called "non-subject parameters" as a limiting mechanism. For example, the library might restrict from its profile books that are revised editions, or that are collections of essays or conference papers. (This does not necessarily mean that the library has no interest in acquiring such books, only that the library does not want to receive them automatically.) When the vendor has a batch of new books ready for shipment, it filters them according to the library's profile, sending automatically those books that fit the criteria identified by the library, sending notifications of books that are on the periphery of the library's identified interests, and neither shipping nor notifying the library of those titles that are excluded from consideration by the profile. Such arrangements are called "approval plans" because, as originally constituted, they provided the automatically shipped books on approval: Library customers would examine the books upon receipt, keep those they wished to buy, and return the rest to the vendor. (Over time, however, most libraries' approval plans have become so refined by this process that they no longer want or need to return any of the books that are sent automatically.)

The *subscription* is the usual method of acquiring scholarly content published in journals: The subscribing library pays a fee at the beginning of each subscription year, and then receives all issues of the journal published that year. Closely related to the subscription is the *standing order*, an instruction to a book publisher (or jobber) that all books published in a particular series should be sent automatically to the library. (Less common is the *blanket order*, by which the library instructs a vendor to send every book produced by a particular publisher.)

The central importance of collection development to the identity and value proposition of the traditional library cannot be overstated. Indeed, the concept of the collection is intrinsically bound up in the concept of the library—the two terms have always been, to a real degree, synonymous. The main reason the library was valuable was that it offered access to scholarly documents that its patrons otherwise would not be able to have, and that it made those documents accessible both by organizing, housing, and curating them and by providing assistance in finding one's way around the collection and deciding which sources to use. The idea of a library without a collection—a carefully and professionally built, vigorously vetted, consistently organized, and rigorously managed collection—would have been as absurd to earlier generations as the idea of a hospital without medical equipment or a restaurant without food.

However, one of the more important and disruptive changes brought by the advent of the Internet has been the radically increased discoverability it creates for documents of all kinds. The combination of metadata (of which library catalogs, with their descriptive records, represent one type) and full-text searchability has made it so that online documents are now discoverable in ways unheard of only a generation ago. Those who grew up and went to school prior to the 1980s will recall that in the old days, the only way to find a book in the library was to search for it in a physical card catalog. For each book in the collection, the library catalog would have multiple cards: one with the title at the top (followed by full bibliographic information below), one with the author's name at the top, and then multiple other cards with subject terms at the top. These cards were all filed alphabetically by the bibliographic element at the top of the card. Thus, if you were looking for a book by Pete Seeger called *How to Play the Five-string Banjo*, you would find it in the catalog by looking under "Seeger, Pete," or by looking up the title "How to Play the Five-string Banjo," or by looking up the subject heading "Banjo—Method—Self-instruction," or "Folk Music—United States." Each of these cards would indicate the call number of the book itself, which allowed you to locate the library's copy on its shelf in the stacks. Although many of us (especially librarians) feel a pang of nostalgia when we remember the days of the card catalog, no one should be deceived: This system was a necessary evil, one that made access to scholarly documents possible but was also confusing, time-consuming, and frustrating. (Library catalogs are now almost universally online, where many, though not all, of the difficulties of card catalog searching have been eliminated.)

Furthermore, in the pre-Internet days it was not only difficult to gain access to books one knew existed, but it was relatively difficult even to learn of their existence. One learned about the publication of new books primarily through ads in newspapers and magazines (there was no e-mail marketing, no Amazon, no Pinterest) and by word of mouth. What this meant was that *discovery* and *access* were very tightly connected, and both tended to take place in the library. In other words, if one wondered "Is there such a thing as a book on banjo playing?" one would usually try to answer it by searching the catalog of one's local library or consulting with the librarian. If one already knew that such a book existed and wondered whether a copy was accessible, the strategy for getting an answer to that question was effectively identical.

The Internet has changed both strategies radically. Now, the question "Is there such a thing as a book on banjo playing?" can most easily and effectively be answered by a quick keyword search in Google or Amazon. Once the book's existence has been established, the question "Is a copy of *How to Play the Five-string Banjo* easily available to me right now?" might best be answered by recourse to one's local library catalog. And this brings us to what has probably been the most revolutionary change to library collection development in the history of the profession: the invention of demand-driven (or patron-driven) acquisition.

What is demand-driven acquisition?

The advent of the Internet has changed academic library collecting strategies in two fundamental ways: by allowing scholarly content to be both discovered and consumed online, and by making it possible for libraries to offer books to their patrons that have not actually yet been acquired for the collection, and to then acquire those books instantly and without obvious intermediation when patrons use them. This system is sometimes called patron-driven acquisition but is increasingly referred to as demand-driven acquisition (DDA).

Here is how it works: A publisher or more often a third-party book vendor provides electronic catalog records for e-books that are available but have not yet been purchased by the library. Because there are many more e-books available at any given moment than any library could afford to acquire, and because many of the available e-books will fall outside a particular academic library's collecting scope, some kind of filter or profile will generally be applied to the universe of available e-books, thus limiting the number of records provided to the library for inclusion in the catalog. Nevertheless, the record batch may include thousands or even tens of thousands of titles—many more than the library could or would want to purchase. These books are then discoverable in the library catalog and look to patrons no different from the e-books that have been preemptively purchased by the library; what the patron experiences is simply a much larger collection than would have been available if the collection consisted only of titles selected and bought by librarians.

When a patron comes across an e-book made accessible in this way, purchase will be triggered in different ways depending on the vendor. Under some arrangements, a certain number of accesses will trigger a library purchase: Thus, the first one or two times a library patron accesses the book, there is no charge, but on the third use the library is charged the price of the book and it thereafter becomes a permanent part of the library's e-book collection. Some models discriminate between types of use, allowing an unlimited number of brief views but triggering a sale when a patron navigates multiple times between pages or prints up part of the book. Still other models employ "microcharges" leading up to an ultimate sale: Thus, the first and second uses of an e-book (of whatever the type or duration) might generate a charge equaling 10% of the book's full price, with the third use triggering a sale at full price, at which point the book becomes a permanent part of the library collection and no further charges are imposed.

The attentive reader will have noticed that DDA models turn the traditional mode of library collection building completely on its head: Instead of librarians selecting and curating a collection of materials chosen for the purpose of meeting local research and teaching needs, DDA puts a much larger and radically less selective list of books in front of the library patron, ultimately retaining only those that are actually used. (Under most DDA programs, e-book records cycle into and out of the library catalog on a regular but infrequent basis, the unused titles eventually going away to be replaced by new ones.)

It is important to note that DDA does not require library patrons to select books, or to make deliberate or conscious choices about what the library should and should not acquire. It does not turn patrons into librarians. The DDA model simply responds to the actual scholarly work that library patrons do. Ideally, they are never aware of the inner workings of the DDA model at all—they simply do their work, and if they notice any difference at all in their library experience as a result of the adoption of DDA, it should only be the experience of a dramatically larger collection of e-books than they would otherwise have had access to.

What are the pros and cons of DDA?

It may come as no surprise to most readers that DDA is a somewhat controversial model among librarians, for a number of reasons.

For one thing, although DDA does not technically turn patrons into librarians or ask them actively and deliberately to shape the library collection, it certainly does give patrons an unprecedented amount of control over the shape of the collection, however unconsciously and unintentionally they might wield it. DDA does indeed take a significant degree of control over the collection away from librarians, and the inevitable result will be a collection that is less carefully built, less systematic, and less coherent than a completely librarian-built collection would be. It is understandable that a librarian whose training, experience, and passion have led him into the subdiscipline of collection development might object—not only from a selfish standpoint ("If patrons are selecting our books, then what is my job?") but also from a principled belief that a coherent and well-crafted collection is more desirable than one shaped by the whims of patron behavior.

On the other hand, one might well ask why the academic library exists in the first place. Is its primary purpose to curate an outstanding collection, or to support the teaching and research of the host institution? If the latter, then it is important to see the collection as a means rather than an end—and it may be that a relatively less coherent and less carefully crafted collection actually fulfills its function better, if what shapes it is the real-world work of local scholars. Surely there is an argument to be made that a collection that fails to meet the real-world needs of those scholars is, to a very real degree, a failure even if it is outstanding by the standards of traditional librarianship.

Another danger that comes with the territory of DDA is the potential for budgets to be spent in an uncontrolled and unsustainable manner. What if you put $500,000 worth of e-books in front of your patrons at the beginning of the budget year and their use generates $200,000 of purchases in the first month? Let us turn to that issue next.

How do libraries manage budgets in a DDA environment?

One of the most common concerns expressed about DDA arises from the fact that, when it comes to e-book budgets, it puts the library's patrons in the driver's seat: The more books they use, the more the library spends, and the less they use, the less the library spends. How can this possibly be sustainable, especially in an environment of strictly limited (and often shrinking) resources?

The first part of the answer to this question has to do with profile building. No library's DDA plan offers access to the complete universe of available e-books. Instead, e-book titles are usually filtered to some degree by treatment (mostly academic vs. popular), by publisher, by topic, and so forth. This filtering process limits the number of books made available for discovery and purchase on a DDA basis, and thus puts a ceiling on the amount of money that can be allocated to these books as the result of patrons' research behavior.

Of course, since it is a central feature of DDA that it makes available much more content than traditional library purchasing would be able to offer, even a selective array of e-books is going to represent many more titles than the library could afford to purchase, which means that establishing a profile represents the beginning, rather than the end, of the budget management process in a DDA environment. On an ongoing basis, libraries typically engage in some form of *risk pool management*, which simply means managing the number of books available for use. By monitoring the flow of money into DDA purchases, library staff can see whether that flow is sustainable: Is the money on track to be spent by the end of the year, is it looking like the whole year's budget will be spent within the next quarter, and so forth? If money is being spent too quickly, reducing the number of books available will slow the expenditures; if it is being spent too slowly, making more books available will tend to speed expenditure up.

Risk pool management can occur at the subject level as well. If the library sees anomalous patterns of acquisition in one subject area for some reason and believes that these patterns represent an anomaly of some kind (rather than being a genuine reflection of unusually high demand in that area), it can temporarily remove all the books in that area while the staff investigate.

As discussed above, this sort of approach tends to undermine the coherence and stability of the library collection—books show up and disappear unpredictably, and might do so more often in one subject area than in another. Furthermore, with a DDA system there is no guarantee that books will be added to the permanent collection according to any overarching strategy, or even any rhyme or reason apart from the current needs and interests of the library's patrons. These are downsides that libraries have to consider and measure against the upsides of making more content available, of reducing the amount of money spent on books that will not be used, and of building a collection that more accurately reflects the current needs and interests of the library's clientele.

What do publishers think of DDA?

As one might expect, DDA presents a mixed bag of upsides and downsides for publishers, especially for those that focus on academic works with relatively small and specialist audiences.

On the one hand, when libraries are able to put a much larger selection of books in front of their patrons than they would be able to buy preemptively, this gives the niche publisher a greater chance of getting its products in front of potential readers (who, under a DDA model, can create actual sales by using those books). DDA gives libraries a mechanism for broadening enormously the range of titles they make available to their patrons, and this represents a distinct benefit for niche and specialist publishers.

On the other hand, when libraries refrain from actually paying for books until those books are used, this puts niche publishers at a potential disadvantage as well. A book on a relatively obscure topic that the library might, in the past, have purchased due to its high quality and general topical relevance to institutional needs (but which might have rarely or never have been used) may well not be used by a patron during the time that it is made available in the catalog through the DDA plan, leading the publisher to lose a sale that it might have had in the past.

This complexity points up an important philosophical quandary around DDA: To what degree should relevance and usefulness drive library purchasing? What about scholarly quality? If more and more libraries implement acquisitions programs that reward scholarly publishers for producing books that are immediately useful, what will become of the scholars who work in disciplines and subdisciplines that are not so obviously relevant and useful? We will encounter these difficult questions again later, when we discuss some of the challenges and opportunities in university press publishing.

Can DDA work in the print environment?

DDA has arisen in the context of e-book purchasing for the obvious reason that it is most clearly feasible in the online environment: E-book metadata can make the book discoverable in a library catalog without the book being purchased ahead of time, and once discovered, the online environment makes it possible for access to be provided at the click of a button and the purchase consummated instantly, behind the scenes and outside of the patron's experience.

However, the same considerations that would lead a library to embark on a DDA program for e-books (a desire to make more content available, to reduce spending on low-use or unused books, to create a collection that more tightly reflects patrons' needs and interests, etc.) apply to printed books as well. The obvious problem is that, unlike e-books, printed books are physical objects that cannot be made to appear instantaneously when the library registers a patron's desire for access. For this reason, traditional DDA models are not an obvious fit for the print environment.

That is not to say that DDA for print does not exist or cannot work to some degree. There are at least three manifestations of what might be called print DDA that one may find currently in practice in academic libraries.

The first, most common, and most widespread of these are the long-established "suggest a purchase" or "patron request" program and the service known as interlibrary loan (ILL). Most libraries have mechanisms in place by which a patron may contact the library and ask it to obtain a needed book that the library does not currently hold. In response to this kind of need, libraries have for many years employed the practice of lending books to each other. Thus, if a patron at the University of Utah needs a printed book that the U of U library does not own, the library might search in an online union catalog (such as OCLC's WorldCat) to determine whether another university library holds a copy of that book. If it does, the library will send a request for an ILL, the holding library will respond by sending the desired book through the mail, and the book will then be lent to the patron at the U of U. ILL is a highly effective program, in that it makes a vastly greater number of books available to patrons than any individual library can offer; it is also, however, a highly inefficient program, in that it requires the patron to wait—usually for days but sometimes for weeks—before getting access to the desired book. Having received the book, the patron is very often allowed to keep the book for only a short time, usually much shorter than the circulation period in her home library, and may not be allowed to extend the circulation period.

Similarly, the "suggest a purchase" program allows library patrons to recommend that their library simply acquire books that it does not yet own; typically, a book that is acquired in response to such a request is then held for the requesting patron so that he can be the first to check it out. This program often requires a briefer wait than ILL does (because booksellers often ship more quickly than libraries do) and almost always results in a standard circulation period (with renewals possible).

It is worth noting here that since the cost of ILL in staff time and shipping can often be as great as (or greater than) the cost of simply buying a copy of the desired book, and since ILL is typically a slower process than outright purchase, many academic libraries are moving in the direction of "buy instead of borrow"—responding to ILL requests by first checking Amazon or other online booksellers to see whether it would be cheaper and more effective to treat the ILL request as if it were a "suggest a purchase" request.

A second manifestation of what might be called print DDA is the increasingly common practice of on-demand printing employed by publishers and third-party book vendors. From the library end, this looks just like any other kind of book purchasing; however, the difference for the publisher and the distributor is enormous. Print-on-demand means that vendors can fulfill orders without maintaining warehouse stock (with all of the waste and economic loss that model entails). Third-party book vendors like Ingram have what amount to in-house printing presses in their warehouses, which allow them to make deals with publishers whereby orders for their books are received and the books printed and shipped the same day.[1] Publishers like Oxford University Press have embraced this technology,[2] allowing them to revive their backlists and, perhaps more importantly, their out-of-print titles—in fact, the existence of print-on-demand technology makes possible an eventual world in which the very concept of a book being "out of print" can be abandoned, a reality that would benefit everyone involved in scholarship.

Of course, print-on-demand that is realized at a great distance from the library solves only part of the access problem. Like traditional ILL and "suggest a purchase" programs, it makes a much larger number of books available to the patron, but does not make most of those books available in the moment they are needed: Patrons must submit their requests and then wait for the books to be delivered to them. Even the fastest and most efficient such service requires a wait of at least twenty-four hours, and usually at least several days.

However, another kind of print-on-demand technology has emerged in recent years, and this one represents the third (and in many ways most exciting) manifestation of what might be called print DDA: in-house print-on-demand. This service is currently made possible by a single product, though hopefully others will emerge as time goes on: the Espresso Book Machine (EBM). The EBM is somewhat like the industrial print-on-demand equipment housed in the warehouses mentioned above, except on a much smaller scale. It consists, essentially, of two printers connected by a small assembly device, and the whole mechanism is run by a computer that is connected to a networked database of e-books that have been formatted for on-demand printing. When a book from the database is selected, one printer prints out the textblock (or the internal pages of the book) while the other prints a cover on heavier stock. When the textblock has been printed, the assembly device applies glue to the spine, attaches the cover, and trims it to size. After a few moments to allow the glue to dry, the printed book is dropped through a chute into the waiting hands of the requestor.

Obviously, the EBM represents a potential game-changer both for libraries and for publishers. For libraries, it offers the possibility of making an almost unlimited number of books available to patrons, and not only current publications— because the EBM's network draws on digital scans of books from research libraries around North America and the United Kingdom (see discussion of the Google Books project and HathiTrust, in Chapter 8), it includes public domain titles that are hundreds of years old, some of which exist in only a handful of physical copies (or fewer). The implications of this kind of radical broadening of access for scholarship are simply enormous. For publishers, it not only means that their books need never go out of print, but also poses the intriguing possibility of bypassing third-party vendors and distributors altogether and selling efficiently to libraries, bookstores, and individual readers.

Of course, nothing ever works as perfectly as it should, and as of this writing there remain major hurdles that the EBM must overcome before it can revolutionize library collection and bookselling. One of these is the reluctance of publishers to make their books—especially new (or "frontlist") titles—available on the EBM's network. This reluctance seems to stem not only from a lack of certainty about the impact of EBM provision on overall sales, but also on the fact that EBM-printed books are quite simply not as attractive and sturdy as hardbound books (or even many trade paperback bindings). They are quite sturdy, but not very attractive, and for publishers whose brands are built at least in part on the physical experience of reading their books, the EBM is not yet a very appealing method of distribution and sales—especially for frontlist titles that the publisher is used to selling in hard bindings with dust jackets and printed on relatively luxurious paper.

More fundamental, however, is the problem of metadata. Books cannot easily be found unless they are represented in a catalog or database by good descriptive metadata, and creating that metadata is an expensive proposition. As of this writing, the company that manufactures the EBM and curates its networked database of titles has not yet found a cost-effective way of making that database effectively searchable; the metadata records that exist are, in a great many cases, rudimentary at best and inaccurate at worst, effectively making the books in the system unfindable by end users. This has severely hampered the EBM's effectiveness as a discovery and delivery system for printed copies of e-books. If and when this particular problem is overcome, it will mark the end of a significant barrier to the provision of printed books on demand and in real time.

How has the role of libraries changed over the past forty years?

While today's libraries continue to fulfill the three important functions outlined above, the evolution of the scholarly communication ecosystem has significantly changed some of the ways in which they do so. This evolution has brought new opportunities for libraries even as it has challenged some of what have previously been understood to be core functions and values of the library.

For centuries, the ways in which libraries brokered access to content changed very little: Brokering access meant buying physical objects (like books and journal issues) into which information had been encoded by means of ink on paper. Because these documents were physical objects, they could be bought and sold like physical objects; once the library purchased a book it became the library's property and taking care of it became the library's sole responsibility. While copyright law constrained what could be done with the book's intellectual content, it was up to the library to determine how it would manage and care for the object itself. And, significantly, once the book was paid for and delivered, the library's relationship with the supplier ended (with regard to that particular document, anyway).

When it came to journals and other serial publications purchased by subscription, the purchase actually marked the beginning of an ongoing relationship between the library and the publisher or vendor, and that relationship had to be managed. Subscription payments were usually made up front on an annual basis, and the library had to monitor the subscription's ongoing output to ensure that the publisher or vendor was fulfilling its obligations—Has the current issue of the journal been delivered on time? Are we missing any issues?

Over the past couple of decades, however, the location of scholarly documents like books and journal articles has moved substantially out of the physical realm and into the online realm. As discussed earlier, this means that increasingly, "buying" a "copy" of a book does not mean actually acquiring a physical object; it means purchasing the right to access the content of that document online—or, effectively, establishing a subscription. This, in turn, means that the moment of purchase marks the beginning of a library–vendor relationship, not the end of one, and when the library pays for access, the vendor takes on the responsibility to provide that access for the duration of the license.

Another important way in which libraries are changing represents another manifestation of scholarly communication's dramatic shift from the physical to the online realm: Libraries are increasingly content creators and publishers in addition to being purchasers of content created by others. This is the topic of our next question.

What is "library publishing"?

The advent of the Internet has made it possible for libraries not only to work with publishers in new ways, but also to become publishers themselves. This development has manifested itself in at least two significant ways in recent years.

First, universities that operate university presses are increasingly deciding to make the university press a part of the library organizational structure, with the press director reporting to someone in the library (usually the library dean or director). In these circumstances, the library itself may be more or less involved with the publishing activities of the press itself, but in most cases the library is not deeply involved. The reporting line moves into the library, but the press continues to operate as a functionally independent operation. However, in some cases the library and the press can become much more functionally integrated, creating new kinds of cooperative publishing programs.

One example of how this can happen is exemplified by Lever Press, a cooperative publishing enterprise established cooperatively by the University of Michigan Press, the University of Michigan Libraries, and a consortium of liberal arts college libraries.[3] Lever Press is designed to publish institutionally funded open access (OA) e-books with a focus on subjects aligned to the missions of liberal arts institutions, and its funding comes largely from money pledged by participating libraries.

Another way in which libraries can become publishers is by simply . . . becoming publishers. Depending on how loosely one defines "publishing," the Internet has lowered the barriers of entry into publishing almost to the ground. If you want to write a book and make it freely available to all, you can open up a free blog account online and post each chapter as a blog entry. And of course, if you can publish yourself that way you can publish others as well. In Chapter 12 we will discuss institutional repositories (IRs) and mention briefly that they can serve as a publishing platform for "platinum" OA journals (i.e., OA journals that are supported by institutional subvention rather than article processing charges levied on authors). A growing number of libraries are experimenting with this model of library publishing. In a way, it can be seen as a deluxe version of institutional archiving: Not only is the contributed content archived and curated in a publicly accessible online space, but it is also given in-house editorial scrutiny and formatted and branded as a formal publication. This approach has proven especially useful for journals of undergraduate student research and scholarship: An in-house, IR-based journal can offer a valuable first experience with the rigors of academic publishing. But libraries have had success with professional IR-based journals as well; for example, as of this writing the Texas Digital Library hosts nearly fifty journals using the Open Journal Systems platform, some of them peer-reviewed scholarly journals, some of them journals of student research, and some of them professional society publications.[4]

There is another way in which libraries are exploring becoming directly involved with publishing, and that is by working cooperatively with established publishers to change existing publishing models, usually for the purposes of making access to scholarly content freely and openly available to all. One example of such an initiative is the Sponsoring Consortium for Open Access Publishing in Particle Physics (SCOAP3), an international consortium of libraries, funding agencies, research organizations, and other entities that cooperatively underwrite the publishing costs of ten scientific journals, mostly in fields related to high-energy physics.[5] The journals continue to be published by their owners, but the SCOAP3 funding allows the publishers to make the content available to readers at no charge. Under this arrangement libraries are not exactly functioning as publishers per se, but they are taking on a new role by helping to provide direct, external subventions for publishing.

Given the strong appetite for scholarly publishing reform in the library world (and, distributed less evenly, within academia as a whole), as time goes on we can likely expect to see some forms of library publishing continue and thrive, others wither and pass away, and new forms emerge on a regular basis.

How are libraries working to improve the scholarly communication ecosystem?

In the twenty-first century, libraries can be seen most conspicuously to be engaged in attempts to improve the scholarly communication ecosystem by their involvement with and advocacy for OA. But librarians have (and continue to be) actively involved in other ways as well. Some of these include the following.

Serving on publishers' advisory boards

While this kind of service can be controversial within the profession (some of whose members see it as a bit like giving aid and comfort to the enemy), many librarians serve on publishers' library advisory boards. The arguments both for and against doing so are fairly obvious: On the one hand, why should we help publishers (especially for-profit commercial ones) figure out how best to get our money? On the other hand, unless we plan to stop buying their products altogether—which at least some librarians do think would be a fine idea—why not help publishers make their products better and help them understand better the challenges and issues facing libraries? Ultimately, the decision whether or not to serve on an advisory board is one of both strategy and conscience. It can also be a matter of policy: Some libraries and their campuses, in the interest of minimizing conflicts of interest, place very strict rules around participation on the advisory boards of external companies; others might allow librarians to participate, but do not allow them to accept an honorarium, or let the company cover travel expenses to board meetings, or even pay for meals.

Doing and publishing original research on issues related to scholarly communication

Librarians (both as individuals and as groups) regularly contribute to the academic study of the scholarly communication ecosystem. There are hundreds of scholarly journals, magazines, and newsletters dedicated to the practices of librarianship and scholarly publishing, and librarians regularly publish research studies, essays, and reviews in such outlets as well as others. Library organizations (notably the Association of Research Libraries, but many others as well) also subject the ecosystem to various kinds of analysis, tracking trends in library funding, collection sizes, expenditures on different kind of published materials, developments in the publishing world, and so forth, and distributing the results of that analysis (often, though not always, at no charge) to the other members of that ecosystem.

Contributing to the development and propagation of publishing and reporting standards

Here we are getting somewhat into the weeds of wonky scholarly communication nerdiness, but standards— though often, and perhaps ideally, transparent to many members of the community—can make a very big difference in the lives of scholars and scientists. For example, librarians were instrumental in the establishment of the Counting Online Usage of Networked Electronic Resources (COUNTER) standard in 2003. This standard codifies a system of usage reporting for online resources like journals, databases, e-books, and reference sources.[6] Since libraries' decisions about renewal or cancellation of these resources are informed substantially by usage data, COUNTER is an example of a standard that has a direct impact on the experience of working researchers. Several hundred libraries and library organizations are members of the National Information Standards Organization (NISO)'s Library Standards Alliance, in which capacity they help to develop standards that are applied by libraries, publishers, and other information creators and providers throughout the scholarly communication community.[7] And of course, you have librarians to thank—or to curse—for maintaining the standard system of call numbers that tell you where to find books on the shelves in your local library.

Working for broader and freer access to scholarly information

While the open access movement is controversial in a number of ways (see Chapter 12 for a fuller discussion of the complexities around this important topic), there is no question that it represents an important way in which libraries, among many other entities, are trying to improve the scholarly communication ecosystem. The basic idea behind this movement is that everyone ought to have free and unfettered access to scholarly publications. Journal and database subscriptions in scientific disciplines can cost thousands of dollars—and, in some cases, tens of thousands. Those without access to a research library generally cannot afford to buy access to such publications for themselves, and even those with access to such libraries often have less access than they would like, due to continually rising journal prices and relatively stagnant library budgets. By supporting and helping to develop programs and policies that make scholarship freely available to all both to read and to reuse, libraries seek to overcome those barriers on behalf of their own patrons and of others.

What are "digital libraries" and what relationship do they have to traditional libraries?

The term "digital library" can have a variety of meanings, depending on the context.

In the broadest sense of the term, a digital library can be almost any collection of documents that are stored in digital formats. These documents may be "digital native" (i.e., originally created by means of computers), or they may have their origins as analog documents that have been subsequently digitized. This book, for example, is an example of a digital native document—you may be reading a printed version of it, or you may be reading it in an electronic version for Kindle or in some other digital format, but it was written on a computer and is thus an example of a "digital native" document.

In recent years, there has been a proliferation of digital libraries of various kinds. These include:

- HathiTrust (a library of digitized books from various research library collections, about which there is more discussion elsewhere in this book)[8]
- The Digital Public Library of America (a discovery tool that does not house, but rather provides links to, a wide-ranging and decentralized collection of

digitized and publicly available documents including books, maps, photographs, and other resources)[9]

- Project Gutenberg (a collection of over 50,000 digitized and digital native books)[10]
- The American Memory Project (a collection of digitized text, sound, and video documents from the Library of Congress and other public institutions—and one of the first such collections ever put on the Internet)[11]
- University-based digital collections, usually based on their libraries' special collections (about which more below). Notable examples of these include the California Digital Library (much, though not all, of which is freely available to the public),[12] the North Carolina Digital Heritage Center,[13] and the Tulane University Digital Library.[14]

What is the difference between libraries' "special collections" and their general collections?

The typical academic library is two very different libraries housed together under the same roof and within the same organizational structure. Because of this organizational arrangement, the fundamental differences between them are not always obvious—but those differences are dramatic and important.

The library's general collection—which may also be referred to as the "circulating collection," the "main collection," and sometimes even the "commodity collection"—will consist primarily of books and other documents that are neither rare nor highly valuable (in strictly monetary terms). These books, recordings, and other resources are usually the kinds of documents that anyone might be able to purchase in a bookstore or online: novels and works of general nonfiction, scholarly monographs, compact discs, maps, journal issues, and so forth. They are selected for acquisition and retention not because they need special protection and curation, but because they meet the teaching and research needs of the campus, and when presented in physical formats they are typically kept in open shelving (i.e., shelving that is located in public areas of the library where anyone may come in and browse them) because the risk involved in making them easily available to the public is relatively low. If one of these documents is lost or stolen, it can usually be replaced at a minimal cost, and if one of them is damaged and cannot easily be replaced, it can be repaired without impacting the value and utility of the document. A very important feature that the materials in the general collection have in common is that their value lies primarily in their function as *containers* rather than as *objects*—in other words, they are important because of the information they contain, not because they have any special value as physical artifacts. In other words, if the library loses its copy of a 2005 edition of John Steinbeck's *East of Eden*, the loss is not likely to be significant because it is relatively easy to find and purchase a replacement of that particular printing—and if that edition is out of print, another edition may serve the library's purpose equally well. These, then, are what we might call "commodity documents"—documents that are of primarily utilitarian value to the library and its users. The commodity collection, as a whole, is tremendously important (indeed, it is arguably central to the library's value proposition), but each individual document in the commodity collection is not usually of great monetary value or significance in and of itself.

The library's special collections present a near mirror image of the general collection in just about every respect. Whereas the documents in the general collection tend to be mass-produced and available for purchase in the standard retail marketplace, those in special collections are often rare and sometimes unique, and are bought and sold in specialist markets. Where the value of a commodity book lies primarily in its intellectual content, the main value of a special collections title will often lie in its significance as an artifact—which means that it may well be irreplaceable, and if it were damaged, repairing it might actually have a negative impact on its value. For this reason, books in special collections are usually kept behind locked doors (and sometimes in climate-controlled vaults) and access to them is very carefully supervised and managed. Consider, for example, a signed first edition of *Lord of the Rings* by J.R.R. Tolkien. While the text of the book—its intellectual content—may be exactly the same as that of any other first edition, the fact that it is a signed first edition makes the book rare and highly valuable, possibly worth thousands of dollars. No library would knowingly place such a copy in its open shelving, because the risk of loss would be very high. If that book were lost, replacing it would be both expensive and difficult.

In many libraries' special collections, there are materials that are entirely unique as well, such as handwritten manuscripts, magnetic tape recordings that exist in only a single copy, original drawings, and so forth. These objects may be very valuable both for their intellectual content and for their properties as unique and irreplaceable physical objects, and they are treated accordingly, with access to them being very tightly controlled.

For rare and unique materials, the promise of digitization and the development of digital collections is especially significant. For example, the University of Utah's J. Willard Marriott Library has a collection of handwritten nineteenth-century diaries written by Mormon pioneers who came west on the Overland Trail. These diaries are valuable both for the information they contain (stories and reflections of Americans who participated directly in the westward migration) and for their uniqueness as physical remnants of an important period of American history. While it would be impossible to make these documents *physically accessible* to more than a small number of people due to their fragility and uniqueness, modern technology has made it possible for the library to make the *intellectual content* of these diaries freely available to anyone with an Internet connection—which that library is now doing.[15] In other words, digital technology now allows libraries to create commodity documents (easily replaceable digital surrogates) out of rare and unique ones. This is something that has only become widely possible in the past decade or so, and its potential impact on the world of scholarship is enormous.

Why do libraries restrict access to and/or reuse of public domain materials in their collections?

Those whose research brings them regularly into contact with research libraries' special collections will have noticed that in many of these libraries, restrictions are placed on how the rare and unique documents contained in those collections may be reused. The restrictions may be expressed in the form of "permission to publish" documents that the researcher is required to sign before being given access, the terms of which require the researcher to ask for permission before republishing the documents in question, or (in some cases) before even quoting from them. Some permission-to-publish documents require the researcher to tell the library where any quotations will be published.

This practice is becoming increasingly controversial in libraries.[16] In some cases it is clearly justified, such as when a donor has (for example) given the library a set of personal diaries under the explicit conditions that they not be published. In such a case, the library is not only justified but positively obligated to notify researchers that the content of those diaries may not be published. However, where the documents in question are not under any kind of donor restriction and are in the public domain, it is more difficult to justify the practice of restricting patrons' reuse of them. It can be difficult to abandon these longstanding practices, however, especially when they generate revenue for the library (by the imposition of reuse fees).

In the online realm, such restriction may be imposed more mechanically, such as by inserting virtual watermarks into digitized photographs (and removing them only upon request or payment of a fee), by making documents visible online but not downloadable, or by providing only thumbnail versions online.

It should be noted that there is a significant philosophical difference between charging a cost-recovery fee for the on-demand digitization of rare and unique documents and charging a "use fee" for the reuse of already digitized content or for published quotation from physical documents. In the former case, the library is being reimbursed for a service that it otherwise might not be able to afford to provide; in the latter case, the library is charging patrons for exercising a privilege with regard to content itself.

It is worth noting that in imposing such restrictions, libraries are typically acting well within their legal rights. A photograph may be in the public domain, but that fact does not obligate the library that owns the photograph to share it. The question here is not one of legal rights, but of professional ethics: Is it ethical for a library to impose restrictions on the reuse of public domain materials? There is not widespread agreement among librarians as to how that question should be answered.

*Why don't academic libraries typically provide course texts
for their students?*

This is a question that has become more complicated and
fraught in recent years.

First of all, it should be noted that library practices
with regard to textbooks vary from place to place. In
some countries, it is fairly common for university libraries to collect textbooks and make them available to students. In the United States, however, academic libraries
typically do not maintain collections of textbooks. There
are exceptions to this rule: The North Carolina State
University Libraries, for example, work with the local
campus bookstore to acquire "at least one copy of every
required textbook and make them available on Reserve"
each semester.[17] However, in the United States such exceptions are rare. Why is that?

There are several possible explanations. One is that
throughout most of the history of higher education, textbooks (like books generally) were published in print format. At a comprehensive or research-intensive university,
the logistical challenge of maintaining a collection of all
required textbooks would be massive. Doing so would
require not only dedicating a large amount of shelf space
to the textbook collection, but also securing that space (to
prevent theft by unscrupulous students), and perform-
ing a complete audit of course offerings, required reading
lists, and the existing textbook collection every semester
or teaching period. At the end of each semester, the library
would have to remove dropped textbooks and add new
ones—a process that would require more or less constant
communication with faculty, who, it is fair to say, are not
universally known for their timely responsiveness with
regard to course text adoptions. The logistical challenges
would be significant.

While the logistical problems of housing and managing a comprehensive textbook collection go some way toward explaining most academic libraries' reluctance to undertake such a service, another explanation is the sheer expense that the service would entail. Course texts tend to be more expensive than other scholarly books; in some disciplines, it is not unusual for a course text to cost several hundred dollars. On a university campus with tens of thousands of students and hundreds of courses (many of them taught in multiple sections with a different text adopted for each section), the cost of a comprehensive textbook collection could easily reach into the hundreds of thousands of dollars, with thousands or tens of thousands being spent each semester to keep it updated. Given the tight budgets under which most academic libraries operate, and the plethora of other demands made on those budgets, maintaining a comprehensive textbook collection is fiscally challenging to say the least.

A third explanation is cultural: In the United States, it is simply a well-established tradition that students will buy personal copies of their own classroom texts while the institution will pay for supplemental research materials and provide those through the library. When faced with a demand for library-provided textbooks, librarians have often simply responded by saying, "That's not our job." This response is sometimes merely reflexive and sometimes more thoughtful and strategic, but the cultural aspect of this tradition should not be overlooked.

In light of the fact that textbooks are increasingly available in electronic formats (greatly easing the logistical challenge for libraries, if not the financial or cultural ones), and as libraries increasingly look for new ways to be relevant and useful to their clientele, the possibility of providing textbooks is arising again in the professional conversation. However, many librarians see the solution to the problem of expensive textbooks not in brokering access to expensive textbooks, but rather in fostering the development and provision of open educational resources (OERs).[18] OERs are often (but not always) textbooks and other online resources developed for course adoption, which are free to use. Sometimes they are developed using grant funds or other subsidies that allow the author to realize a direct financial benefit from the undertaking (in the place of the royalty payments he would get from sales of a traditional textbook), and sometimes they are developed as a labor of love by those who are passionate about the topic and dedicated to the principle of free access to scholarly information. In addition to the challenge of getting OERs created, there is the challenge of convincing instructors to adopt them—academics tend to protect fiercely their right to determine which materials they will use in their teaching and to resist institutional pressure to adopt particular resources, even if those resources will be more affordable to their students. As of this writing, OERs are still a relatively new development in the scholarly communication ecosystem, and it remains to be seen to what degree they will end up displacing traditional course texts—though their potential for disruption seems significant if they reach a critical mass of adoption.

What is the difference between a library and an archives?

And now that you mention it, what is the difference between an "archive" and an "archives"? The answer to that second question is relatively simple, though not entirely without controversy: Generally speaking, archivists, librarians, and other information professionals will refer to a particular collection of archival materials as an "archive" and to the organization that houses archival materials as "an archives." Among other things, this usage serves to distinguish between more traditional archival institutions and the various kinds of online archiving that have become widespread with the development of the Internet. We follow that convention in this book.

The first question—about the difference between a library and an archives—is a little bit more complicated. Libraries and archives are similar in some very obvious ways: Both of them collect documents, organize them, take care of them, and make them available for use by those whom the organization exists to serve. However, beneath those surface similarities lie a few fundamental differences. Those differences can perhaps best be summed up as the gap between a focus on *access* and a focus on *preservation*.

While both libraries and archives provide access and perform a preservation function, the balance between these two areas of focus is, in libraries, almost the mirror opposite of what it is in archives. For a library, access is the overriding goal: libraries buy and take care of books and journals, and license access to online content, so that patrons will have the freest possible access to as much desired content as possible. Where restrictions on access are imposed, it is always in order to serve the access needs of the whole community. For example, your library might allow you to renew a checked-out book only once; the purpose of this policy is not to reduce your access to it, but to maximize others' access—the restriction represents a compromise designed to make access as broad as possible. Similarly, most libraries put their physical collections out on shelves that can be freely browsed by the public, and even by people who might not be entitled to check the books out. This practice represents a sacrifice of preservation in the interest of access: Unintermediated physical access to the books greatly increases the risk that they will be damaged, but in the library this is considered an acceptable risk because the library's primary goal is not to protect books, but to expose them to use.

In an archives, on the other hand, preservation is paramount. Archives are often attached to corporate entities of various kinds, as well as to political communities (like cities and towns) and academic communities (like colleges and universities). The primary contents of an archives will usually be papers and other documents that embody the corporate history of its parent organization. They may be used for research purposes, for example by someone writing a company history, but their primary function is to help the organization continue to do its work effectively (by providing information about past dealings with other companies or about sales history, for example) and to comply with regulatory requirements or professional standards. For this reason, access to archives tends to be very tightly controlled and restricted: A corporation's archives will contain a lot of information that is strategically or legally sensitive, and not everyone in the company (let alone outside of it) will have access to it. Corporate archives are almost never browsable; access to them tends to be heavily mediated.

As explained above, the "special collections" area of a research library represents something of a hybrid between library and archival functions.

7

THE ROLE OF UNIVERSITY PRESSES

How did university presses come into existence?

University press publishing has its origins with two of the first universities in the Western Hemisphere: those at Oxford and Cambridge. Both of those universities were printing books and other scholarly documents on a relatively small scale by the middle of the sixteenth century, and the practice of university-based scholarly publishing grew slowly and had expanded into North America by the early nineteenth century. In 1919, there were thirteen university presses operating in the United States, and as of this writing there are hundreds in operation around the world.[1]

To many of us today, university press publishing is nearly synonymous with the scholarly monograph. However, university presses often publish journals as well, and in the latter part of the twentieth century there was a significant increase in the number of "trade" books published by university presses. These are books aimed at more general and less scholarly audiences, often with a regional focus. Regional cooking, travel, ethnic studies, and regional political history are examples of topics that are likely to be treated in university press trade titles, and these often provide much more robust sales than those yielded by scholarly books—sales that, in many cases, underwrite the production of scholarly monographs.

What makes university presses different from other scholarly publishers?

The most obvious difference is that university presses are almost always sub-organizations of universities. (There are a few publishing organizations that call themselves "university presses" but are not actually affiliated with any university—the University Press of America is one example, though as of this writing it has not published any books in recent years and appears to have been discontinued as an imprint by its parent company, Rowman & Littlefield.) Because university presses are usually established as part of the research and teaching mission of their parent institutions, they do not always seek to turn a profit—nor are they necessarily expected to. Some are established as cost centers and operate on a subvention basis, and simply do their best not to cost the institution too much. Others have the goal of breaking even, while others—a few—have become highly successful commercial publishing entities in all but name. Of this last category, probably the best and most well-known example is Oxford University Press, which is a department of the University of Oxford but at the same time a multinational corporation with thousands of employees and surpluses in excess of $150 million per year.[2]

A more important distinguishing characteristic of university presses is the kinds of books and journals that they publish. As mentioned above, university press output is characterized significantly by scholarly monographs—academic books on highly specialized topics written by scholars for a primary audience of other scholars. University press books are less likely than trade books to be found in public libraries but have historically been acquired in large numbers by academic and research libraries. Scholarly monographs also tend to be more expensive than trade books and, due to their specialized nature, are often printed in runs of under a thousand copies.

In some disciplines, especially in humanistic fields like history and literature, university press books may be revised versions of scholars' doctoral dissertations. This reflects another very important function of university presses. In such disciplines, junior faculty may be required to publish at least one book with a scholarly press (preferably a university press) in order to secure tenure. A faculty member in this situation might use her doctoral dissertation as the basis for her first monograph, a fact that has implications for the storage and dissemination of the dissertation itself. (Some of these implications are discussed further in Chapter 12 on open access.)

How do university presses select books for publication?

Unlike generalist trade presses, most university presses focus their publishing efforts on a particular subject area (or a small cluster of subject areas). These subjects often have a regional dimension. Thus, for example, the University of Minnesota Press is particularly well known for its publications in social and cultural theory, urbanism, and feminist criticism (among other related fields). It also publishes books on the natural and cultural history of America's upper Midwest, reflecting its geographical location and cultural milieu. An author who wishes to publish a scholarly monograph on Appalachian string band music or on the history of kingship in Hawai'i is not likely to succeed at getting his book published by the University of Minnesota Press—not because those are unworthy topics or because the book is not well written, but simply because it is in the nature of most university presses to have a fairly well-defined scope of subject coverage. This dimension of selectiveness has to do with relevance rather than scholarly quality.

Scholarly quality is another centrally important selectivity factor for university presses, however. Because their mission is more academic than commercial, most university presses seek to publish books that will make a significant contribution to knowledge in the author's academic discipline—even if those books are not likely to sell very many copies. This does not mean that university presses are unconcerned with sales; on the contrary, even those that are not expected to turn a profit still hope to publish books that will be read by many and have a broad scholarly impact. It does mean, however, that university presses tend to select manuscripts for publication according to criteria other than expected popularity.

The mechanisms by which university presses review book proposals and decide which ones to accept will vary from press to press, depending significantly upon staff size. Generally speaking, university presses employ acquisitions editors who, in consultation with the press director, make final decisions about which book proposals to accept and which ones to decline. In many cases, editors are helped in their initial culling of the proposals by an advisory board made up of local faculty and other interested scholars, all of whom provide input to the editors to help them make the first cut. Book proposals themselves may arrive at the press unsolicited, or may be invited or commissioned by the press from an author with whom the press is interested in working.

Of course, once a book proposal has been accepted and the manuscript submitted, there are still hurdles to overcome before the book is finally published. Many university

presses employ a peer-review system both when considering book proposals and to review submitted manuscripts
prior to final acceptance. This system is designed to do very
much the same thing as what happens with peer review of
scholarly journal articles (as discussed in Chapter 4): It creates a layer of expert review that is not just editorial but
also draws upon the discipline-specific expertise of the
author's colleagues. For authors, the benefit of this system
is not just that their work is improved by virtue of rigorous
vetting, but also that it increases the brand value of their
publication. To be published by a press known for the rigor
of its peer-review process is to have a significant feather in
one's scholarly cap.

Do university presses publish books on a subsidy basis?

To answer this question, we must introduce the concept of
subsidy publishing, and then we must briefly revisit the
question of what a "university press" really is.

First of all, it is important to note the difference between
"subsidized publishing" and "subsidy publishing."
"Subsidized publishing" is a term sometimes used to
describe an arrangement whereby the press is funded by
another entity, and may or may not be expected to realize profits or surpluses from its publishing activity. Some
university presses operate under this kind of arrangement;
instead of being expected to make their own way in the
commercial marketplace, their costs are covered by their
host institutions, with the expectation that they will publish books and other materials that support the institutional
mission.

"Subsidy publishing"—which is sometimes more pejoratively called "vanity" publishing—is an activity whereby
the publisher accepts whatever manuscript is offered by an

author, sometimes (but not always) offering some degree of editorial oversight and intervention, and requires the author to cover the costs of the resulting book's publication. The charges may take the form of an upfront subsidy, which is to say that the author pays some amount of money up front in return for the printing of a specified number of copies, or the author might be required to buy enough copies of the final book to cover the publisher's costs and provide some degree of surplus. Obviously, there is nothing intrinsically wrong with this business model; under such an arrangement, the publisher is simply a service provider and is neither offering nor pretending to provide the kind of vetting (whether for marketability or for scholarly quality or both) that is an important part of the traditional scholarly publishing transaction.

This arrangement only becomes controversial when a subsidy publisher presents itself in the marketplace as a conventional scholarly enterprise, and represents its books as the products of a conventional process of scholarly discrimination and editorial oversight. In recent history, a number of putatively academic publishers have attracted negative attention in the scholarly world for what is alleged to be just that kind of behavior. Some of these publishers have proven quite litigious, so their names will not be mentioned in this book. However, an Internet search on the terms "vanity," "scholarly," and "publishing" will lead the interested reader to quite a few discussions of this topic.

As for what constitutes a "real" university press, here the issues are less contentious but still not entirely straightforward. As mentioned above, there have been publishers calling themselves "university presses" despite not being affiliated with any university. The University Press of America was one such; Edwin Mellen University Press published monographs as recently as 1997, despite the fact that its sponsoring institution was a short-lived university headquartered in the Turks and Caicos Islands that offered degrees based on life experience. Neither of these publishers is exactly what most people have in mind when they think of "university press publishing," and yet there was nothing to stop them from calling themselves university presses. The definitional boundaries of the term are maintained not by statute or regulation but by professional norms.

There is a professional organization for university press publishing: the American Association of University Presses (AAUP). Not all of its members are actually university presses (members include the American Historical Association and the Brookings Institution, for example), but if a publishing house calls itself a university press and is also a member of AAUP, it is certainly a true university press.

Does anyone actually read scholarly monographs?

This may seem like a frivolous or dismissive question at first blush, but it is in fact one with which authors, publishers, and libraries have been struggling for decades—and with increasing urgency in recent years, as library budgets have tightened in response to economic downturns and readers' behaviors have shifted with the profusion of new options. But the issue of audience and market has been with us for as long as scholarly publishing has existed. It requires us to think about questions of value and cost, questions that are particularly difficult in the context of scholarly communication. How do we measure the value of an idea or argument? If the idea is very original and forward-thinking, it may draw a very large number of readers by virtue of its originality and novelty, or it may draw no readers at all because it seems outlandish or silly and unworthy of attention. Should a press make its acquisition decision based on what it believes to be the quality of the argument, or based on the size of its anticipated audience? One obvious answer would be that these criteria are not mutually exclusive, and that the press should consider both—which is easy enough to say, of course, but fiendishly difficult to apply in practice.

One important problem is the fact that a book's audience is determined not only (and maybe even not primarily) by its quality but also to a substantial degree by its relevance to potential buyers and readers. This is true for individuals as well as for libraries. The world's best monograph on Bhutanese architecture may—despite its excellent quality—be of interest only to a small number of individual readers, and of relevance only to the work of a few scholars (and therefore arguably not a wise purchase for many libraries). A mediocre book on the basics of market economics may—despite its middling quality—be of interest and usefulness to a much larger number of readers. It is easy to see which book has the larger natural audience, but which of them is the more valuable? (For more discussion of the interaction between quality and relevance in scholarly book publishing, see Chapter 10.)

In other words, the objective value of a book is difficult to determine, and is ultimately subjective, because it is determined by factors other than objective measures of quality. The *quality* of a book does not vary by context, but its *value* does. But even if it were possible to determine a book's value in a rigorously defensible way, the problem of cost would remain: For every 100 high-relevance and high-quality books that are made available in the marketplace, an interested individual may only be able to afford one. And even research libraries, despite having book purchasing budgets thousands of times larger than those of most individuals, cannot afford to purchase or house all of the books that might conceivably be useful to the students and faculty they serve.

These are issues with which individual book-buyers struggle as they decide which books to purchase for their own use, but libraries struggle with them even more desperately because they are trying to support the teaching, learning, and research of anywhere from hundreds to tens of thousands of individuals with widely disparate tastes, interests, and backgrounds. In the contexts of these struggles, the question "Does anyone actually read scholarly monographs?" takes on a heavy significance.

The simple answer to the question, of course, is "Yes," but its simplicity is misleading. A more accurate answer would be, "Yes, most scholarly monographs get read by at least one person, although it depends on what you mean by 'read.'" And here we encounter another dimension of difficulty with this question: What does it mean to "read" a scholarly monograph? If the question is "How many people read a scholarly monograph from beginning to end?" the answer is going to be a fairly low number—despite the fact that this is how such books are usually designed to be used. If the question is "How many people consult a scholarly monograph in the course of their research, looking for information relevant to their work on a related topic?" the answer will be a much higher number. Indeed, it has long been the case that books in academic libraries are very frequently used more as databases than as books—as repositories of information, some of which may be brought to bear on a question, rather than as immersive journeys along the path of a linear argument.

While the book-as-database scenario may not be the use anticipated (or desired) by authors, it is a scenario that makes the audience for scholarly books quite a bit larger than it would otherwise be. It also suggests an argument in favor of making scholarly monographs available as e-books, a format much more suited to interrogative research use than the bound codex is.

What is the place of university presses in the open access movement?

The development of open access (OA) models for books has been slower than it has in the world of journal publishing. This is partly because the demonstrable reader demand for journal articles (especially in the science disciplines) tends to be quite a bit stronger than it is for monographs, and so the pressure created by demand on toll-access models is greater in that domain. However, it is also because the cost of publishing a monograph is so much higher than the cost of publishing a journal article. According to one recent study, the total cost of publishing a scholarly monograph is typically somewhere in the neighborhood of \$27,000.[3] By contrast, if the article processing charges of Gold OA journals are any indication, journal articles in the applied and social sciences generally cost between \$1,000 and \$3,000 to produce. This means that in addition to the lower reader demand for access to scholarly monographs, there is also a greater cost barrier to providing it—while the combination of greater demand and lower production cost per unit creates relatively low barriers to free access when it comes to journal articles.

There is nothing particularly surprising about these cost differentials, given the differing size and complexity of monographs and journal articles and the difference in the amount of research and intellectual effort required to produce them. Those differences, along with the relatively small audiences for most scholarly monographs, do go some way toward explaining why it has taken longer for OA solutions to emerge in the realm of monographs.

Nevertheless, OA book publishing models are indeed emerging, and seem to be doing so with increasing speed in recent years. Some notable examples of these models are discussed in Chapter 12.

What is the future of the university press?

The current scholarly communication environment is a turbulent one for university presses; many of the things about scholarly publishing that have changed radically over the past few decades, and that continue to change, have a direct impact on the viability of the university press. Nor is there any reason to believe that the rate of change is going to slow in the foreseeable future, or that the ongoing volatility of the scholarly communication ecosystem is going to make it more congenial to university presses as they are currently conceived.

For example, circulation rates in research libraries have been on a precipitous decline since at least the early 1990s.[4] To the degree that academic libraries continue to be important customers for university presses, and to the degree that libraries' buying practices are shaped by their patrons' behavior with regard to books, it is difficult to see this trend portending anything good for university presses. Indeed, as discussed in the previous chapter, academic libraries are quickly moving in directions that connect patrons' reading and research habits directly to collection development, and therefore involve the purchase of fewer books (in all formats) than was the case in the past.

Another area in which things are changing quickly has to do with organizational structure. An increasing number of university presses are being subsumed into the libraries of their host universities. In 2014, a survey by the AAUP found that 17.5% of university presses were reporting to a library dean or director—that is nearly one in five, and more have made this transition since.[5] It is worth asking why this is happening; indeed, significant voices in the scholarly communication world (notably that of publishing consultant Joe Esposito, who wrote a thoughtful piece on this topic in the *Scholarly Kitchen* blog[6]) have argued against it. The answers will vary from place to place, of course. The answers seem to fall into two broad categories, however: the *defensive* and the *proactive*.

The defensive argument for bringing the university press under the library's umbrella is simply that, in order for it to continue fulfilling its mission, the press needs protection from market forces that threaten it. With book sales falling, the press will go under if left out in the cold marketplace on its own, and the library provides shelter: a stable infrastructure, access to a larger pool of institutionally allocated funds, and (politically speaking) integration within an organization that is understood and expected to be a cost center rather than a revenue-generator. From this perspective, the library is a safe harbor. In a 2016 interview with *Inside Higher Education*, University of Michigan Press director Charles Watkinson put it this way: "One of the amazing things of being integrated into a library is at least it's given us some breathing room. . . . We don't always have to look over our shoulder for that next dollar. It gives presses the capacity and freedom to innovate and, perhaps on the revenue side, dig themselves out as well."[7]

Watkinson's comments provide a nice segue from the defensive argument ("We don't always have to look over our shoulder for that next dollar") to the proactive one: "It gives presses the capacity and freedom to innovate." This is, for many participants in this trend, the much more exciting argument in favor of library–press mergers. From this perspective, what makes the absorption of a press into the library attractive is not so much what such a move prevents as what it makes possible. At Michigan, the library–press merger has resulted in the creation of Lever Press, a new scholarly book publishing initiative that involves a consortium of presses and libraries at liberal arts colleges.[8] At the University of Utah, the university press's integration into the library has facilitated the revival of access to a long-out-of-print series of archaeological papers, all of which can now be printed on demand using the library's Espresso Book Machine. Similar (and very different) programs are emerging in other academic libraries as they absorb and collaborate with university presses.

8

GOOGLE BOOKS AND HATHITRUST

What is the Google Books Project?

Google Books has its origins in an idea that occurred to Google founders Sergey Brin and Larry Page in the mid-1990s, when they were graduate students and the World Wide Web was still in its infancy. They imagined a world in which massive numbers of print books would be digitized, and people could use search engines to easily index and analyze their content. The original idea was to digitally scan *all* of the world's books, but the project began at a more manageable level: with partnerships forged between Google and the research libraries at Harvard, the University of Michigan, and Stanford, as well as New York Public Library and Oxford University's Bodleian Library. Crucially, partners also included a number of important scholarly and trade publishers, including Blackwell, Penguin, Houghton Mifflin, Springer, and Taylor & Francis—and university presses at the University of Chicago, Oxford, and Princeton.[1]

Over time the project expanded, and Google's team worked its way through the book stacks at dozens of major academic, national, and public libraries, scanning their book holdings page by page and creating a digital copy of each book. In return for giving Google access to its collection in this way, each library received a digital copy of every book from its collection that was scanned, effectively creating for each library a digital version of its existing physical collection at no direct cost to the library while giving Google a massive database of digitized text.

How many books are contained in the Google Books collection?

Exact numbers have not been officially released, but in 2015 the *New York Times* reported that Google had scanned "more than 25 million volumes" in total, "including texts in more than 400 languages from more than 100 countries."[2]

Hang on. How can it possibly be legal for a commercial firm to engage in systematic, wholesale copying of in-copyright books for use by the public?

That is a great question, and it will not come as a surprise to the attentive and thoughtful reader that the Google Books project was controversial from the beginning. Copyright holders (both authors and publishers) got upset as soon as they got wind of the project, and lawsuits were filed quickly. In 2005, the Authors Guild brought a class action suit against Google on behalf of authors, claiming that Google had failed both to respect copyright and to fairly compensate authors for the use of their work.[3] At the same time, five commercial publishers and the Association of American Publishers (AAP) brought a separate civil suit against Google, also claiming copyright infringement.[4]

The Google Books project faced international obstacles and objections as well. In France, where copyright laws are unusually strict by international standards, a coalition of French publishers successfully sued to have Google's project shut down with respect to copyrighted books published in France, including those housed in U.S. libraries.[5]

However, the lawsuits that were brought against Google in the United States were not as successful as the French ones; in fact, they were ultimately not successful at all. At first, Google and the plaintiffs attempted to come to a negotiated settlement. A joint settlement of both the Authors Guild and the AAP lawsuits (which had been consolidated in 2005) was proposed in 2008; it provided for Google to make a payment of $125 million to the plaintiffs and laid out licensing terms that would allow Google to sell access to the digitized books both to individuals and to institutions on a subscription basis. The settlement was rejected by the courts on the grounds that it might violate U.S. antitrust law. The parties submitted an amended settlement agreement a year later, but it was rejected in 2011. (Google reached a separate settlement with AAP in 2012.) Finally, the lawsuit itself was rejected in 2013. The plaintiffs appealed the rejection in 2014, but in 2015 the appeals court unanimously upheld the original finding in Google's favor. The plaintiffs' subsequent appeal to the Supreme Court was denied in 2016.[6]

Why did the courts ultimately find in favor of Google, when it might seem obvious that the massive and systematic copying of in-copyright books flies in the face of copyright law?

First of all, a fundamental question for this lawsuit was whether the digitization of these printed books represented a "transformative" use. It is important to understand that copyright law draws a distinction between reproduction that results in a "slavish copy" (a simple and straightforward copy that creates nothing new or original) and reproduction that somehow transforms the original into something meaningfully new. In their lawsuit, the authors and publishers made an argument that seems pretty reasonable on its face: Google was not doing anything meaningfully transformative with its digitization project—it was doing nothing to these books except creating digital copies of them. Google added no interpretation, no new text, no new content. However, Google's argument was that by making *digital* copies of the printed books, it was transforming them into documents that could be used in radically new ways (for purposes such as text-mining and analysis, aggregated full-text searching, etc.) and that could be made available to those with reading and visual disabilities in ways that are not possible with print. The courts found that argument compelling and explicitly sided with Google on this point.

Second, it ended up being significant that Google had agreed to make the texts of the digitized books *searchable* but not *fully readable* online. This had very significant implications for the fair use argument. (See further discussion of the concept of "fair use" in Chapter 5.) The Google Books project did not actually take millions of in-copyright books and put them up on the open Web for all to read for free. Instead, it turned those millions of books into a massive database of text that can be searched freely—but the results that come back from those searches are snippets that provide enough text to give the search results some context, but not enough to replicate the experience of actually having access to the book. Google argued (convincingly, in the court's eyes) that providing this kind of access to the in-copyright texts would have no impact on the market for the books in question and could even drive sales by helping readers locate books in which they might be interested. And Google also argued that this kind of use is transformative.

It is also worth noting—as the court did—that the vast majority of the books digitized by Google were works of nonfiction. This fact has a significant bearing on questions of copyright infringement as well, since factual works are entitled to less stringent protection than creative ones.

All of these points of analysis, among others, led the court to conclude that the Google Books project constituted fair use of the copyrighted works, despite the fact that it involved the systematic and wholesale copying of entire works and the exploitation of those copies for commercial purposes.

Apart from the finding on fair use, however, the court also laid out in some detail the significant public benefit that it saw in the Google Books project. While public benefit itself is not sufficient either to justify copyright infringement or to define copying and redistribution as fair use, in this case the court found that the public benefit aspect of the use combined with a strong fair use argument in a compelling way. In the closing comments of his decision, Judge Denny Chin put it this way:

> In my view, Google Books provides significant public benefits. It advances the progress of the arts and sciences, while maintaining respectful consideration for the rights of authors and other creative individuals, and without adversely impacting the rights of copyright holders. It has become an invaluable research tool that permits students, teachers, librarians, and others to more efficiently identify and locate books. It has given scholars the ability, for the first time, to conduct full-text searches of tens of millions of books. It preserves books, in particular out-of-print and old books that have been forgotten in the bowels of libraries, and it gives them new life. It facilitates access to books for print-disabled and remote or underserved populations. It generates new audiences and creates new sources of income for authors and publishers. Indeed, all society benefits.[7]

The bottom line, then, is that after years of consideration, negotiation, and public and private dispute, the courts ultimately ruled that the Google Books project was legal and legitimate. It was a landmark moment in the legal history of copyright, and one that the advent of the Internet had probably made inevitable, though the specific outcome of these particular lawsuits was not.

How can I use Google Books?

As mentioned above, most digitized books in the Google Books corpus are not available for online reading or download; their content can be searched for words or phrases, and the results of such searches will reveal the location of the search terms in various books but in most cases will not permit the searcher to read the entire volume. How much of each book's content is made available in the search results will vary from title to title, depending on the nature of the work and Google's agreements with the copyright holders. In many cases, it is possible to read as many as several dozen pages, but the viewable pages are often scattered throughout the book's text. For researchers, however, this kind of access can be tremendously valuable; being able to thoroughly interrogate the text of a book (rather than being forced either to read the entire text or rely on the crude approximation of full-text searching provided by conventional indexing) not only makes many traditional forms of research much less time-consuming but also enables new kinds of research that were simply impossible during the print era.

One example of a research tool made possible by mass book digitization projects like Google Books is the Google Ngram Viewer. In computational linguistics, the term "n-gram" refers to a string of letters or characters identified within a larger corpus of text (such as a word or phrase in a book). The Google Ngram Viewer allows researchers (or the merely curious) to see how many times a given string of characters occurs within the Google Books corpus, displaying their frequency by year.[8] Since the Google Books corpus includes books published as long ago as the early 1500s, this tool can provide interesting evidence for the first emergence of words and phrases in the published literature and their change in prevalence over time. While the Google Books corpus is neither comprehensive nor representative enough to provide a perfect index of that literature, it is large and representative enough to yield search results that are interesting and suggestive at the very least—search results that, again, could not have been achieved otherwise.

While it is true that most of the books digitized by Google are not available for comprehensive online reading, there is a significant exception to that general rule, and it pertains to books that are in the public domain (and therefore not subject to copyright restrictions). Where public domain books have been digitized as part of the Google Books corpus, they are made fully and freely available for reading and download.

What is HathiTrust?

When Google partnered with American research libraries to create its corpus of digitized books, it left behind at each library a set of images based on the digitization it had performed in that collection. This meant that when Google took its scanning machinery and moved on, each of those libraries was left with what amounted to a complete (or nearly complete) digital copy of its book collection—and in many cases, this meant millions of e-books.

At that point, it was not yet clear what could legally be done with those digital copies—the various lawsuits against Google had not yet concluded, and in fact some had not yet been filed—and the copyright issues were (and remain) complex. One thing was clear, though: These digital files needed to be organized, curated, and preserved, and this was a project better approached by multiple institutions cooperatively than by each of them individually.

Thus was HathiTrust born. Taking for its brand the Hindi word for elephant (a symbol of size, density, and long memory), HathiTrust was initiated as a collaborative partnership between the member libraries of the Committee on Institutional Cooperation (which consisted mainly of large research libraries in the American Midwest) and those of the University of California system. These libraries pooled their resources to create a shared repository for their digitized collections, with an emphasis on not only preserving but also making available the content of those collections. Once the HathiTrust organization was off the ground, it began inviting other libraries and research organizations to join as well; as of this writing, the partnership includes five library consortia (or state systems) and 118 individual libraries and research institutes in five countries.[9] Also as of this writing, the HathiTrust collection includes over 5 billion pages of text in just under 15 million volumes (representing about 7.3 million unique titles, since some of the books are multivolume works). Of those volumes, roughly 39% (or 5.7 million) are in the public domain. The HathiTrust corpus continues to grow as member libraries contribute digitized content from their own collections.

The range and diversity of content available in HathiTrust are astounding. Its holdings include books in no fewer than 460 languages—and that alone is something to think about. HathiTrust includes books not just in English and Serbian and Hungarian and Wolof, but also in Truk, Divehi, Altai, and Adygei. As for HathiTrust's coverage in time, the earliest publications included in the corpus were published prior to 1500 and the most recent is from 2009. The pre-1500 imprints number nearly 20,000, all of which, obviously, are in the public domain and therefore fully and freely available to anyone with an Internet connection.

It is worth considering the significance of this development for both the present and the future of scholarly communication. The rise of the Internet in recent decades has made many of us fairly blasé about having free access to an effectively unlimited wealth of information. Not only has the Internet allowed us to get quick and nearly effortless answers to simple questions ("What time is it in Cairo?"; "What does a mongoose look like?") but it also makes it possible for us to conduct fairly sophisticated research in very short periods of time. However, most of what is available for free online is not scholarly information; most of it is popular, even demotic, and much of it is ephemeral. What HathiTrust has created, for the first time in human history, is a scholarly research tool the likes of which was previously unavailable even to scholars at the world's top universities—and it is freely available to anyone with an Internet connection. Furthermore, it has created a free online library of millions and millions of books that anyone may read, and a significant number of which can be freely downloaded as well. Think only of the 20,000 pre-1500 books contained in HathiTrust: No single research library in the world contains that many books from that period, and they are now all available to be read and downloaded by anyone with an Internet connection. The implications of this development for scholarship are truly amazing.

Did HathiTrust run into legal issues similar to those experienced by the Google Books project?

It most certainly did. In 2011, the Authors Guild (along with several other organizations and some individual copyright holders) brought suit against HathiTrust (along with the presidents of several member universities), arguing that its creation of a huge digital archive of titles from the Google Books project constituted the "systematic, concerted, widespread and unauthorized reproduction and distribution of millions of copyrighted books and other works," thereby "risking the potentially catastrophic, widespread dissemination of those millions of works in derogation of the statutorily-defined framework governing library books." The plaintiffs' fundamental argument was that the systematic digitization of these books, and HathiTrust's subsequent use of them to create a searchable online archive, "far exceed(ed) the express limitations of Section 108 (of the U.S. copyright law), which cannot be excused by fair use under Section 107."[10]

The plaintiffs took particular umbrage at what HathiTrust was calling its Orphan Works Project. (See Chapter 5 for an explanation of the concept of "orphan works" under copyright.) This project—planned but not yet fully undertaken at the time of the lawsuit—would have taken books that were under copyright but for which the identity of the copyright holder was not obvious, and made them freely available online to affiliated users of the libraries that had donated them to the archive.[11] Importantly, the plan included a provision for copyright holders to identify themselves and issue takedown requests.

The Orphan Works Project would have been administered by the University of Michigan, but after the suit was filed, Michigan shelved the project indefinitely.[12] However, over the next several years the plaintiffs suffered a series of legal defeats, culminating in a 2012 dismissal of the lawsuit,[13] a dismissal that was upheld on appeal.[14] Although the lawsuit was dismissed, the Orphan Works Project remains in limbo as of this writing, possibly because of the risk that starting it up again would generate a new lawsuit—one that might not be as easily or resoundingly won as the original was.

9

NEEDS AND PRACTICES IN STM AND HSS

What do STM and HSS stand for?

STM stands for "scientific, technical, and medical," and the acronym has basically come to be used as a shorthand reference to what many call the "hard" sciences—those that produce findings based on controlled laboratory practice, concrete experimentation, and experimental data. In contrast, HSS stands for "humanities and social sciences," or, in other words, the arts and humanities along with the "soft sciences"—those that rely more heavily on subjective interpretation and analysis, even when their work is significantly data-driven. What are referred to as the "soft sciences" usually involve the study of human behavior: psychology, economics, sociology, and so forth.

Unsurprisingly, the terms "hard" and "soft" science are somewhat contested. The term "soft" can easily come across as derogatory (and, indeed, it is sometimes—though not always—intended that way). Economists and social psychologists will argue that their work is based on rigorous modeling and controlled experimentation, while an STM researcher might respond that the results of those models and experiments are nonetheless open to subjective interpretation in a way that, say, physics or chemistry experiments simply are not.

This is a debate that has gone on for a very long time and will probably never end—partly because it is largely philosophical (a "what do these words 'really' mean?" argument) and therefore difficult to resolve in any absolute way, and partly because the stakes can be quite high, making it difficult for either side to concede ground. The world of grant funding is a viciously competitive one, and government agencies and other grant-makers are under increasing pressure to demonstrate the real-world impact of their investments of taxpayer and endowment dollars. Because the STM disciplines very often produce concrete deliverables with clear and easily explained value propositions (e.g., effective drug treatments, efficient car engines, bridges that do not fall down), those in HSS fields who often produce results that have less of an obviously practical value (e.g., insights into the behavior of populations, ballets and symphonies, analyses of poetry) are increasingly at a disadvantage, and recent trends in government funding both in the United States and the United Kingdom have given humanists and social scientists ample reason for alarm.[1] Public debate will continue to rage as to how we ought to measure the relative value of the sciences and the arts and humanities, and that debate remains important.

What are the differences between STM and HSS scholarship in practice?

STM and HSS researchers use different tools in the pursuit of different kinds of results. For example, in many STM disciplines, research is conducted in laboratories. Laboratories provide both specialized equipment and tightly controlled experimental environments. The concept of "control" is a very important one here: It refers to a scientist's ability to isolate the variables being tested from other, "intervening" ones that might confound or contaminate the results of the experiment and their relevance to the hypothesis under examination. So, for example, a researcher investigating the effects of a particular bacterium on mice would carefully isolate the mice from an environment in which other bacteria might influence the result. Another aspect of control lies in the use of "control groups" for comparison. Thus, the experiment on mice will be considered more valid and rigorous if the results for an "experimental group"—the mice who are exposed to the bacterium—can be compared to those for a control group that is not exposed to it. Such an approach lowers the likelihood that the bacterium's observed effects are actually the result of something other than exposure to the bacterium.

HSS researchers also employ widely accepted research methodologies in their work, including the use of experimental and control groups, but they will also often make use of qualitative data, such as survey instruments that require research subjects to explain their feelings or attitudes; interviews with subjects (the results of which must obviously be interpreted by the scientist); measurements of group dynamics, which are only meaningful when given some kind of interpretation by the researcher; and so forth. Furthermore, HSS research very often consists of the study of things that cannot be observed directly, and the existence of which may even be controversial. For example, the nature of the mind and the degree to which the mind exists as an entity separate from the brain are questions that have vexed both philosophers and scientists for centuries, and yet entire HSS disciplines are built on the assumption that the mind exists and that it can be studied scientifically. Economics is a highly quantitative HSS discipline, but making economic data meaningful necessarily involves drawing inferences about human attitudes and behavior—and those inferential leaps can at times be heroic.

It is worth emphasizing here that we should be careful about equating concreteness with usefulness or quality. Economic models and psychological research have both proved tremendously useful in everyday life and have advanced our understanding of ourselves, each other, and the world around us in important ways, as have laboratory experiments and direct measurements of natural phenomena. Both the STM and the HSS disciplines have also produced useless, poorly understood, and disastrously misused research results.

One of the important functions of the scholarly communication system that has developed over the past centuries is to provide a filter that pushes bad research to the margins and showcases good research, whatever the discipline. The system performs this function imperfectly, of course—it is difficult to imagine a system that would not—but it is important to bear in mind that this filtering and sorting is a large part of what scholarly communication is about.

Do scholarly communication practices differ significantly between the STM and HSS disciplines?

In some ways they do, and in others they are quite similar. One thing that both the STM and HSS disciplines have in common is a strong cultural norm in favor of peer-reviewed publication. The mechanics of traditional peer review are discussed in some depth in Chapter 4, but here it is worth repeating that peer review creates a layer of assessment and scholarly oversight between the author and the journal or book editor. Since no editor can be an expert in every area of her discipline, and since, even if she could, conflicts of interest might arise (e.g., a submitting author might be a personal friend, or might work for a company for which the editor is a consultant), having trusted and expert third parties available to provide a dispassionate (and traditionally anonymous) critique can be invaluable to ensuring the quality of research presented by the journal or book publisher. Of course, not all quality journals are peer-reviewed, and not all scholarly monograph publishers employ peer review. But it is common for tenure committees and other evaluators in both the STM and the HSS disciplines to look specifically for peer-reviewed publications when evaluating the performance of junior faculty.

A very important difference between the STM and the HSS disciplines lies in their respective cultural expectations regarding publication type and format. A rule of thumb in the HSS disciplines is that a junior faculty member will not get tenure unless he has published at least one monograph with a reputable scholarly publisher (usually a university press) during his early years on the tenure track. This rule is not universal, but it is generally applicable. A young scholar's first book is often—though not always—based on his doctoral dissertation. (For more discussion of the intersection between publicly available theses and dissertations and formal publication, see Chapter 12.) In the STM disciplines, however, monographs are less important— here, the "coin of the realm" is the peer-reviewed journal article, and the prestige of the journal in which an article is published matters very much. (For more on the prestige market in academic journals, see Chapter 4.)

10

METRICS AND ALTMETRICS

*How is quality defined and measured in the world
of scholarly publishing?*

The concept of scholarly quality is a complicated one
because it has multiple dimensions that apply in different ways depending on the type of publication in question
and the context in which it is being evaluated. It is also
difficult because *quality* and *relevance* are both important
criteria that guide purchase and use decisions for readers
and libraries, but they do not describe the same variables.

For example, consider a scholarly book on the topic of
nineteenth-century German architecture. Imagine that this
book is, in fact, the best one ever written on that topic. An
individual who is doing research on sociology or botany or
physics may have no need for that book, despite its excep-
tional quality.

Now imagine a thoroughly mediocre scholarly book on
nineteenth-century German architecture. An individual
who is doing comprehensive research on the literature
of architecture, or a library that supports a world-class
architecture program and needs to offer researchers in
that program a comprehensive collection of books on the
topic (even if some of them are not truly great books) may
need access to that book regardless of its less-than-stellar
quality.

Both of the above scenarios show how, in some scholarly use cases, relevance can trump quality—and the effect of relevance trumping quality may be to make a book either less necessary or more necessary.

Interestingly, it is less common for quality to trump relevance—both for individual readers and book buyers and for libraries. An individual reader with no interest whatsoever in architecture is not likely to buy a copy of the world's best architecture book, and a library is not likely to purchase the world's best architecture book unless its collection development staff have reason to expect that it will get at least some use. (For more discussion of how libraries make decisions about which books and journal subscriptions to buy, see Chapter 6.)

The same is true for journal and database subscriptions: Both individuals and libraries will take the quality of a title into account when deciding whether or not to acquire it, but the trump card is usually relevance rather than pure quality. A major difference between journal and database subscriptions and book purchases, of course, lies in the fact that the latter involve ongoing commitments of money rather than one-time purchases. This means that whereas the decision to purchase a book is usually made only once (and may be regretted later but cannot really be reversed), the decision to subscribe to a journal or database is made annually and can be revisited with each renewal. If it turns out that the subscription decision was a poor one, the individual or library can cancel the subscription and stop paying for it.

OK, granted that quality and relevance are not the same thing, the question remains: How do participants in the scholarly communication ecosystem measure quality?

We can answer this question in a general way by looking at two broad categories of scholarly publication: books and journal articles. The quality measures applied to each are somewhat different. Later in this chapter, we will also examine some differences between the ways that authors consider quality (when deciding where to submit their work) and buyers and readers think about quality (when deciding what to purchase).

Two very important signifiers of quality for scholarly books are publisher reputation and book reviews. The reputation of a publisher is significant both for authors seeking to be published and for buyers (especially libraries) seeking to build collections. Particularly in the humanities and social science disciplines, scholarly authors will generally try to get their books published by highly regarded university presses—and this is especially true for early career scholars publishing their first book, since many academic departments set the publication of a monograph with a university press as a baseline requirement for promotion and tenure. But libraries pay close attention to publisher reputation too, especially when they are creating profiles for vendor approval plans. (The question of how approval plans work in academic libraries is also addressed in Chapter 6.) Libraries pay attention to publisher reputation because, generally speaking, it is a fairly reliable rough-cut measure of quality: Just as an author may reasonably expect that publishing a book with Harvard University Press will enhance his career more than publishing it with, say, the University Press of America, so a library may reasonably expect that acquiring a Harvard UP book will enhance its collection more than acquiring one from the UPA. None of this is to say that Harvard UP never publishes mediocre books or that UPA never published excellent ones—but one of them has published more influential and award-winning books than the other, and the track record of each will have an impact on choices made both by authors seeking to be published and by readers and libraries looking for books to buy.

How is a scholarly book publisher's track record of quality established? Mainly by book reviews and, perhaps to a lesser degree, by awards. When a publisher's book list elicits a steady stream of positive reviews in such prestigious publications as the *Times Literary Supplement*, the *New York Review of Books*, or *Kirkus Reviews*, its reputation as a producer of high-quality scholarship grows. And when it publishes books that garner important awards in the relevant disciplines, that also helps to bolster its reputation as a place where authors will want to place their work and as a producer of books that readers and libraries ought to purchase. Of these two factors, book reviews probably count more, because they are a *lingua franca*—just about everyone understands the significance of a positive review in the *Times Literary Supplement*, but not everyone will immediately recognize the significance of the Cundill Prize.

Again, though, it is important to bear in mind that when it comes to books, each purchase is usually a small gamble and an isolated one. The library buys a book with the expectation that its quality and relevance will make it useful to the library's patrons; having made the purchase, no additional spending is required (beyond what it costs to process and care for the book), and there exists no option to return it for a refund ten years later if the book turns out to have been an unwise purchase. In the great majority of cases, books purchased by readers and libraries are relatively cheap (compared to journal or database subscriptions), and this has an impact on buying behaviors as well: Libraries, in particular, are often much more cautious in establishing new subscriptions than in deciding which books to buy.

Do journals employ a different quality metric from that used for books?

Yes, a very different one, and as it turns out the question of measuring journal quality is quite controversial. In the journal realm, publisher reputation plays a smaller role than it does in the book realm—both for authors seeking to place their work and for individuals and libraries considering which journal subscriptions to purchase. Journal publishers typically publish multiple (sometimes hundreds, and in a few unusual cases even thousands) of journals, and those journals' reputations are generally determined at the title level rather than at the publisher level. In other words, it does not usually matter much to a journal's reputation whether it is published by Elsevier or Wiley or the American Chemical Society, though all of those publishers have solid reputations for producing high-quality scholarship. What matters much more is whether an individual journal has a high or low *impact factor* (IF).

The IF is a metric designed to measure the influence that a journal has on its discipline by calculating the ratio of citations to articles and creating a score for the journal derived from that calculation.[1] Each journal thus indexed receives an annual score based on citations to its articles found in the literature during the previous two years. Thus, if a particular journal's articles are cited 1,000 times in 2015, and the journal published a total of 150 articles during the previous two years (2013 and 2014), the IF is calculated by dividing the number of 2015 citations that refer to 2013/2014 articles by the total number of articles that were published in that journal during 2013 and 2014. For the hypothetical journal in question, if 700 of the 1,000 citations from 2015 were to articles published during 2013 and 2014, the journal's IF for 2015 would be 4.666.

It would be difficult to overstate the importance that the IF has acquired in the scholarly realm—especially in the hard sciences—since its invention in 1975. For better or for worse, it has become a widely used shorthand measure of journal quality that influences not only buying decisions in libraries, but also (even more controversially) tenure, promotion, and salary decisions in academic departments, where publishing in journals with high IFs may be expected as a condition of advancement. For this reason, the IF is also a driving factor for authors looking for places in which to publish. This is true in some cultures and disciplines more than in others; in China, for example, it has become fairly common for academic institutions to offer faculty authors cash incentives for publishing articles in journals with high IFs. This is not a common practice in most European and North American institutions, but the ongoing explosive growth in research output from China—and the pressure on Chinese researchers to publish in Western journals—means that practices such as this have a growing impact on the shape of scholarly and scientific publishing practices generally.[2]

This development would not be particularly troubling if the IF were less controversial. However, in recent years there has been a growing chorus of calls for the abolition of the IF, or at least for it to be given much less prominence and importance.

Why is the impact factor so controversial?

The IF is seen as problematic for a number of reasons.

The first is the fact that it is the commercial product of a for-profit company. IFs are calculated and published by Thomson Reuters, which publishes *Journal Citation Reports*, the venue in which IFs are announced every year. IFs calculated by any other entity are considered fake and illegitimate, and in fact there are companies that seek deliberately to deceive with wholly spurious IFs.[3] Furthermore, it is a common practice of predatory or deceptive publishers (see Chapter 13 for more discussion of these) to claim for their journals IFs that are simply made up and have no basis in actual citation history. (A dead giveaway of such invention is when a journal claims to have an IF while still in its first or second year of publication—only in very rare cases can a journal have a legitimate IF prior to the end of its third year of publication.) But for many people, the fact that the IF is itself the commercial product of a for-profit publisher immediately casts a certain amount of suspicion on its validity as a dispassionate measure of scholarly quality.

The second is the fact that a high number of citations is not necessarily a measure of scholarly quality or scientific validity. One of the most serious criticisms of the IF arises from the fact that citations alone do not say anything one way or another about an article's quality, and therefore citation counts are a questionable measure of the actual scholarly impact of the journal in which it is published. For example, an article may be cited 100 times as a sterling example of groundbreaking scholarly insight, or it may be cited 100 times as an example of scurrilous fraud—either way, those 100 citations will have the same (positive) effect on the IF of the journal in which that article was published. This is one reason that the relatively neutral term "impact" is used rather than a more positive term—the IF is not necessarily intended to show that a journal is of consistently high quality, but rather that its publications have contributed to shaping the professional discourse, whether because of their high quality or of their low quality. Inevitably, however, this is not how the IF has come to be commonly seen—it is widely used as an actual measure of quality (see further discussion below). This may not technically be Thomson Reuters' fault, any more than it is a hammer manufacturer's fault when someone uses the hammer to build a shoddy house, but a reasonable argument can be made that it is nevertheless a genuine limitation of the IF itself.

The third problem is the ease with which IFs may be manipulated. Because a journal's IF is determined by citations, and because citations are cheap and easy to generate, artificially inflating a journal's IF is relatively simple. Now, "simple" isn't the same thing as "easy," and someone who wants to game a journal's IF will face the challenge of generating enough citations to have a real impact (no pun intended). It can be done, however. One way is by publishing a high number of review articles (which give an overview of the current state of research on a topic rather than presenting new research); these articles tend to attract lots of citations.[4]

Another way is by offering authors incentives to cite articles previously published in the journal, or refusing to publish their work unless they do so. This is referred to as "coercive citation" and is generally regarded as an especially odious practice among scholars.[5] Coercive citation is one manifestation of the more general practice of journal self-citation, which may be legitimate and appropriate (after all, there is nothing wrong with an author's article citing other articles published previously by the journal in which it appears), but may also be deliberately overused in order to game the prestige system. In 2013, Thomson Reuters excluded 66 scientific journals from the IF calculation for one year as a punishment for excessive self-citation.[6]

Yet another way to game the IF system—though a more risky and labor-intensive one—is to form a citation cartel. This requires multiple journals or editors to collude with each other in encouraging high numbers of citations to each other's journals, whether by encouraging authors to cite papers from those journals or by rejecting papers that fail to cite them.[7]

Other methods of IF manipulation exist as well.

The final problem is the fact that the IF measures a *journal's impact* but is often misconstrued as an indicator of *article quality*. In other words, a journal with a high IF gives a certain reputational sheen to the articles published within it. This is precisely why authors are sometimes given concrete incentives to publish in high-IF journals—the administrators giving those incentives understand that they will have bragging rights if they can publicize the fact that their faculty publish X number of articles each year in journals with IFs of Y or higher. As explained above, the IF of a journal does not necessarily say anything about the actual quality of its articles— more problematic still, however, the IF of a journal does not even necessarily say anything about the *impact* of any individual article published in that journal. Many of the articles in a given journal will be cited rarely or not at all, regardless of how high that particular journal's overall IF is. It is worth noting again that this problem is not, strictly speaking, a problem with the IF itself; it is a problem that arises from people misunderstanding or actively misusing the IF. But it is often given as one reason why the IF should not have the central importance that it has come to have.

Is the IF the only citation-based impact metric in wide use?

No. In recent years others have emerged as well.

For example, the *h-index* is a citation metric that is designed to measure the impact of a particular author in her field by measuring patterns in citations of her work.[8]

This metric actually tracks both productivity levels and researcher impact (as measured by citations, anyway). Although it is intended as a metric of impact for individual researchers, it can also be used to measure journal impact.

Another important citation-based impact metric is the *Eigenfactor*. This metric, developed at the University of Washington by Carl Bergstrom and Jevin West, seeks to measure a "journal's total importance to the scientific community."[9] It does so not only by counting citations but also by giving extra weight to citations from highly ranked journals. This tool also generates article-level rankings, called Article Influence scores, and rankings of author influence. It is the basis for Google's PageRank metric, which measures the importance of website pages.

Are other measurement tools emerging to challenge the primacy of the IF?

Yes, and in fact there has been a movement afoot in recent years that seeks, in significant part, to displace (or at least to supplement) the IF with what its participants believe are better and more valid measures of both quality and impact. Creating new measures of impact has become much easier with the development of the Internet and the nearly wholesale migration of scholarly and scientific publishing into the online realm, and this development is clearly reflected in several of these new measures, which have come collectively to be called "altmetrics."

As explained by Cameron Barnes,[10] "altmetrics are a broad class of statistics which attempt to capture research impact through non-traditional means." These include drawing impact data from such sources as:

- Micro-blogging or short-message services (Twitter)
- Social networking sites (Facebook, Instagram)

- Blogs (WordPress, Blogger)
- Social bookmarking networks (Delicious)
- Academic bookmarking platforms (CiteULike, Mendeley)
- Peer review services (F1000Prime)
- Academic networks (Academia.edu, ResearchGate)
- Collaboratively edited online encyclopedias (Wikipedia)

It is important to emphasize that altmetrics are not typically based on citation counts or patterns. Instead, they seek to measure impact, quality, and importance by other means—and most often, these means involve tracking social behavior and finding quantitative ways to represent it.

One of the emerging altmetrics is *ImpactStory* (formerly known as *total-impact*), which "aims to provide a broader picture of impact to help scholars understand more about the audience and reach of their impact."[11] An author joins ImpactStory and exposes her work to its software, at which point the application searches multiple web application programming interfaces (APIs) in order to detect the impacts of that author's work "along two dimensions: audience (scholars or the public) and type of engagement with research (view, discuss, save, cite, and recommend)." It then assigns a percentile score along each of those dimensions.

Another altmetrics service is *Plum Analytics*, which "uses modern altmetrics to help answer the questions and tell the stories about research."[12] Plum Analytics offers a suite of analysis services including tools to measure the value derived from an institutional repository (see Chapter 12 for discussion of institutional repositories and how they work), the impact of an individual's publications, comparisons of one individual's impact with that of another, the impact of particular research grants, and so forth.

Then there is *DataCite*, which "provides persistent identifiers (DOIs) for research data."[13] While that may not sound exactly like a metrical endeavor, it is important to note that one of this organization's fundamental goals is to "support funding agencies by helping them understand the reach and impact of their funding." In this connection, it is worth bearing in mind that altmetrics are not just about helping scholars and scientists understand how and whether their work is having an impact, or about measuring the impact of journals. Grant-makers, research institutions, and other underwriters of science and scholarship want to know whether the money they are providing to researchers is making a difference, and that desire creates an opportunity for entrepreneurs who are able to create tools that help to determine the real-world effect of publications arising from funded research.

The universe of altmetrics is a highly dynamic one, and products and services in that universe seem to be born and die nearly every month. The question of whether and how scholarly impact can (and whether it ought to) be measured continues to be a controversial one, so this area is likely to remain volatile for the foreseeable future.

Do authors and readers look at "quality" differently?

The answer to this question is complicated, and it ultimately has to be "yes and no." In order to provide an answer, we must refer back to the different reputation dynamics discussed at the beginning of this chapter.

On the one hand, everyone in the scholarly communication ecosystem would likely agree that Oxford University

Press is a reputable publisher of high-quality books and journals. For this reason, authors tend to be eager to place their books with OUP and readers will tend to have relatively high expectations of OUP publications.

When it comes to journals, authors and readers are both more likely to consider quality as a function of journal *title* than of journal *publisher*. For example, the journal *Nucleic Acids Research* is widely considered one of the top journals in chemistry and consequently is one in which academic chemists wish to publish and to which researchers in related scientific disciplines will very much want to have access. It is published by OUP. However, if OUP were to sell *Nucleic Acids Research* to another publisher such as Elsevier or Wiley or the American Chemical Society, that change alone would not be likely to affect the journal's reputation in any significant way. (Of course, if the change in publisher were to lead to the resignation of its editorial staff, then the journal might take a reputational hit—but that would be due to the staff change, not necessarily the change in publisher itself.) As mentioned above, authors often measure journal quality as a function of its IF, though less formal reputational factors come into play as well. In most disciplines, the names of the best journals are widely known, and their desirability as places in which to publish one's papers may have as much to do with that social reputation as with more quantitative measures.

In the cases of both book and journal publishing, however, it is important to remember that what scholarly authors need most from publishers is *certification of quality*—they need to publish their work in venues that will give their work an imprimatur of scholarly merit that is widely recognized and respected in their particular disciplines. Generally speaking, this matters to scholarly and scientific authors more than the size of a publication's readership; given the choice between publishing in a widely read but relatively low-status venue and in a journal that has a smaller readership but a stronger reputation for scholarly quality, these authors will often pick the latter—especially if they have not yet been tenured. This means that questions of quality, impact, and reputation are quite complex and cannot usually be reduced to simple criteria.

11
METADATA AND WHY IT MATTERS

What is metadata?

Literally, the word "metadata" means "data about data," and it refers to a huge variety of information types. A caption printed under a photograph is an example of metadata; so are the catalog record for a library book, a citation to a journal article, and the text that you see when you click "About This Program" in the dropdown menu of a piece of computer software. Basically, if a text serves the primary purpose of describing or referring to other texts or documents, then the main function of that text is to act as metadata.

That may seem like a very simple definition, but it covers a tremendous amount of complexity. For example, there are important distinctions between *descriptive* metadata (which tells you about the informational content of a document), *structural* metadata (which tells you things about how the document is organized), and *administrative* metadata (which tells you things like when the document was created, who is allowed to have access to it, what kind of file it is, etc.).[1]

Of course, these different kinds of metadata can coexist in a single file or document. Thus, for example, the library catalog record for a book in the collection will indicate the title of the book (descriptive), relevant subject headings (descriptive), the date of publication (administrative), the distribution of pages between main text and introductory matter (structural), and information about its physical dimensions and binding (descriptive or structural, depending on how you look at it). If the book in question is an e-book rather than a printed book, and is therefore accessed online, the library's catalog record may also contain an annotation that indicates who is allowed to access it ("Available to university users only"), which would be an example of administrative metadata.

It is also true that metadata records can be applied either to individual documents or to collections of documents, and to all kinds of documents or information objects that are not text-based (photographs, sound recordings, data sets, software, etc.). And—get this—there is even a category of metadata that constitutes data about data about data, and is therefore called (inevitably) metametadata. Thus, a metadata record that indicates the language in which another metadata record is written and when that record was created would constitute metametadata.[2]

By now, the average reader's head may be beginning to hurt, so perhaps we should hurry along to the next question.

Why do we need metadata?

While we have not always used the term "metadata," we have employed metadata for as long as we have tried to organize information—which is to say, for a very, very long time. The library card catalog is one familiar example of metadata (though one with which a steadily shrinking number of people have had direct experience), but there have long been other organizational schemes for collections of documents and tools for wayfinding within them: tables of contents, indexes at the backs of books, archival finding aids, abstracts at the beginning of scholarly articles, and so forth. All of these tools are also examples of metadata, and all of them serve a similar purpose: helping people either locate the documents they need or home in on relevant elements within a document already in hand.

Upon reflection, it will be clear why such information is so important. Imagine being faced with a room full of books that have not been organized in any way—or that have been organized in a manner that is not intuitively obvious (as is the case in most academic library collections, for example). Without recourse to metadata, the only way to find a book of a particular type from within that apparently chaotic mass of information would be to physically examine every book, and the only way to find a discrete piece of information within any particular book would be to read it in its entirety. While many of us will agree that browsing through a book or a collection of books can be a very worthwhile and even pleasurable experience, random browsing is no way to do serious research on a focused topic. Metadata can provide not only context for a document or collection of documents, but also a roadmap to its content.

Metadata also serves the very important function of linking documents together. This is the function of subject headings in library catalog records, for example: If you are looking at a book with the subject heading "Great Britain— Politics and government—1945–1964," you will be able to find other books on the same topic by looking up that subject heading in the catalog. A blog posting will often have a viewable metadata field containing a list of relevant keywords; clicking on any one of those words will bring up a list of other postings from the blog that are tagged with the same terms. On bookstore websites and in online library catalogs, an author's name will almost always be a piece of metadata itself that, when clicked, will bring up a list of records for additional books by that author. And so forth.

What functions do metadata serve in the realm of scholarly communication?

When it comes to scholarly communication, metadata does more than just help people locate relevant or related documents. Particularly in the realm of science and technology, where it is increasingly likely that multiple versions of an article may be freely available online (see discussion of preprint archives and of the "version of record" in Chapter 2), it is increasingly necessary to be able to tell quickly whether the document one sees is the most final and authoritative version. Metadata enables you to make this determination without a word-by-word comparison between what may or may not be two different versions of the same document. In this regard, one of the more important new metadata tools to have emerged in recent years is the Digital Object Identifier (DOI). While the DOI can be applied to many different kinds of information objects (not all of them necessarily digital), its most relevant use for our purposes here is as a persistent and unique identifier for digital scholarly documents, especially online journal articles.[3] The concept of *persistence* is central to the value proposition of the DOI: Whereas an online article might be deleted from the server on which it was originally stored and moved to a different online address (thus resulting in an invalid URL and a dead link), or the ownership of the journal in which it is published might change (resulting in out-of-date metadata), the DOI is based on document attributes that do not change, and can be counted on to serve as a permanent effective link between that document and others that use the DOI as a referent. A DOI is designed never to go out of date.

Metadata tags also make it possible quickly to distinguish between different authors who share the same name, and to forge connections between documents by a single author who might publish under varying forms of his or her name. For example, consider the situation of a scientist named Susan Smith who publishes regularly in the field of biology. Biology is a broad and densely populated scientific discipline, and there are many women in the world named Susan Smith. How can you know whether two articles in biology that credit Susan Smith are the products of the same author? Alternatively, suppose that Susan Smith usually publishes under the name "Susan Smith" but sometimes publishes as "Susie Smith." To help with these kinds of situations, the Open Researcher and Contributor ID (ORCID) was invented in 2012. An ORCID is a bit like a DOI for people: Instead of identifying a unique document or object, it gives a unique tag to an individual who creates documents, thus making it possible to link together all of the documents created by that person.[4]

None of these systems is failsafe, of course (what system is?). DOIs must be created according to strict criteria in order to function as intended, and an ORCID is only as effective as its owner is willing to make it: If a prolific scholar signs up for an ORCID fifteen years into his career and never bothers to attach his ORCID to the articles he published during those previous years, it will not provide a comprehensive link between his various publications. However, the services that both of these tools supply, when they are applied as intended, are becoming increasingly important to the scholarly communication ecosystem.

12

OPEN ACCESS: OPPORTUNITIES AND CHALLENGES

What is "open access"?

Open access (OA) has to do with making access to scholarly content freely available to all. As a term, it is often used in opposition to "toll access," which refers to the prevailing system in scholarly communication now—one whereby people gain access to published scholarship by paying for it, most often in the form of journal and database subscriptions and book purchases. With the dramatic shift of scholarly publishing out of the print and into the online digital realm, OA has become a widespread topic of conversation within the past fifteen years or so; now that so much scholarship is created and distributed digitally, it is possible to think in terms of making it universally available, or at least freely available to everyone with an Internet connection. Whereas the limitations of print formats made it both physically and fiscally impossible to make copies of printed books available to billions of people simultaneously at no charge, the same is obviously not true for networked digital documents, which can be copied and redistributed quickly and easily around the world, and at virtually no incremental cost per copy. (It should be noted, however, that while the Internet has made copying and redistribution of existing documents virtually cost-free, it has not eliminated any of the costs involved in *creating* those documents. More on this below.)

The OA movement also has connections to the "copyleft" movement, in that OA advocates usually encourage the use of Creative Commons licenses (as discussed in Chapter 5). So really, it is useful to think about OA as existing in a couple of different domains of access: It is about making content freely available to *read*, and also about making content freely available to *use*. However, among the large population of people who support OA and consider themselves advocates for it, there is significant disagreement as to the role of reuse rights. (More discussion of this issue will come later in the chapter.)

This brings us to an essential point. It is important to bear in mind that OA is something of a contested term in many ways: Not everyone agrees on its definition, not everyone agrees on the degree to which OA (however defined) should be a universal solution, and not everyone agrees on how OA should be implemented. There is disagreement on these questions both among people who consider themselves to be advocates of OA, and between those who are advocates and those who are uncertain about OA or who are to some degree opposed to it.

What is wrong with "toll access"?

The system often pejoratively referred to as "toll access"— the one whereby those who get access are those who pay for it—is the system of information access that has, for better or worse, prevailed throughout modern history. Authors and publishers have not traditionally made their work freely available for all to read, copy, and redistribute, even if the author's work was underwritten by public funds. For centuries, it was widely accepted that if one wanted access to a book or a journal article, he would have to either pay for that access himself or make use of a library that had brokered access on his behalf. Those without money or access to a library simply went without access to scholarly content.

The downsides of this system are easy to see: Whenever something costs money, those who want it but cannot afford it will go without. The more it costs, the fewer people will likely have access to it. And while this may be a morally acceptable state of affairs when it comes to optional or luxury products like ski vacations and crime novels, it may be more difficult to defend when talking about necessities like food, clean air, and essential (rather than recreational) information.

During the print era—which is to say, the millennia-long information era that began with the emergence of the written word and lasted until the advent of the Internet just a few years ago—it was difficult to make a cogent moral argument for universal free access to scholarly information for the simple reason that such access, however abstractly desirable, was manifestly impossible. Since information was invariably encoded into physical objects, and because physical objects are expensive to create, to transport, to house, and to care for, no reasonable person believed that it was possible to make all scholarly publications universally available to readers at no charge.

However, we no longer live in the print era. Today, the duplication and redistribution of existing scholarly documents can be achieved at virtually no cost. Placing an essay or article on a (free) blog platform costs an author nothing more than the time she invests in dragging and dropping; from there, any one of the billions of people with an Internet connection can read and download it at no direct cost—and redistribute it as well. (Of course, Internet connections do cost money, and there are other small and hidden costs embedded in the system of online communication too. But in comparison to the costs of dissemination during the print era, the direct costs of dissemination in the online era are effectively negligible for most of the individuals involved in it.)

Given that dissemination can now be accomplished at little or no cost, what justification can there be for imposing access tolls between scholarly information and those who want to read and reuse it?

The attentive reader will have noticed that the free distribution scenario proposed above consists entirely of steps taken after the creation of a scholarly product (such as an essay or an article). Obviously, the processes involved in creating that product entail costs that are real, can be substantial, and are always felt directly by the creator. So one response to the question "What is wrong with toll access?" might be "Nothing. Access tolls are about repaying authors for their work, not just about recovering the costs of dissemination." And this is an answer that might be widely accepted in situations where the author's creative or scientific work is undertaken independently and at her own cost. But what about when the general public has either entirely or substantially underwritten that work? Such will be the case, for example, when a scientist is conducting research funded by government grants, or when a literature professor produces a scholarly essay as part of her employment at a public university. In cases like these, is there still a reasonable argument to be made for making the public pay for access to the written results of that work?

Here is where the issues get complex and opinions tend to diverge. Few would deny that it makes obvious sense to say "the public has a right to read the results of research it has funded." But beneath that simple and obvious statement lies a confounding complexity: The public does not typically want access to what it has paid for (a simple write-up of the results of publicly funded scholarly work) but rather to a more refined and vetted version of that product—a version that reflects value added after the fact by entities other than the author or the public. This value is typically added by publishers, and may include such elements as peer review; certification of quality; editorial refinement; formatting; accurate and reliable metadata; reliable archiving; the creation and ongoing curation of active links to referenced works and source data; marketing of the final version to an audience of potential readers; and so forth. Those who defend a toll-access model might argue that if the reading public wants value-added services, it is reasonable for publishers to recoup the cost of those services from the reading public.

Further complicating this issue is the fact that it is not only the reading public who wants these value-added services, but also the authors themselves, for whom formal publication in a prestigious venue may be a sine qua non of professional security and advancement.

But it gets more complicated still. Of the value-added services that publishers provide, many are not provided by the publisher, but rather by unpaid volunteers recruited from the ranks of—wait for it—scholarly and scientific authors. Thus, the costs of producing a peer-reviewed scholarly journal are not borne entirely by the publisher of that journal. Authors of the articles in that journal receive no payment from the publisher; the authors' peers who provide pre-publication review of submitted articles are rarely, if ever, paid for their work by the publisher; even the editors of journals are often—though not always—providing their work without payment.

Why do authors, editors, and reviewers provide their work for free? Partly because such work is considered part and parcel of their academic duties; in other words, it is not so much that they are working for free, but rather that they are being paid by someone else. For authors, it is also because publishing their work in a prestigious journal yields real and concrete career benefits—in academia, publication in well-respected venues is the key to job security. The work of editors and peer reviewers also yields certain career benefits to those who perform it (at tenure time one must be able to demonstrate service not only to the university, but also to one's discipline), and it conveys professional prestige.

So does the fact that content, peer review, and often even editorial services are provided at no direct cost to the publisher fatally undermine any defense of the toll-access system? It depends whom you ask. Publishers will point out the significant costs involved in managing all of these processes; journal publishing is filled with hidden costs, including the cost of rejecting papers (one that cannot be recouped except by surpluses realized elsewhere). Those who categorically oppose toll access will respond by saying that these processes can be managed much more efficiently, and that third-party entities such as traditional publishers are not needed—what we need is a new system that pulls all of the activities around formal publication into the academy, where they will be undertaken by those already being paid to do scholarly work. The resulting publications can, it is argued, then be made available without access tolls.

It is not possible to cover the full range of issues, controversies, and potential solutions regarding access to scholarly information in this chapter, or indeed in this book. Hopefully the complexity and wide-ranging nature of the issues involved is becoming clear, however.

Is there an official definition of OA?

The short answer to this question is "no," but a more accurate answer would be quite a bit more complicated than that.

The most widely accepted definition of OA remains the one formulated by the Budapest Open Access Initiative in 2002:[1]

> By "open access" to [peer-reviewed research literature], we mean its free availability on the public internet, permitting any users to read, download, copy, distribute, print, search, or link to the full texts of these articles, crawl them for indexing, pass them as data to software, or use them for any other lawful purpose, without financial, legal, or technical barriers other than those inseparable from gaining access to the internet itself. The only constraint on reproduction and distribution, and the only role for copyright in this domain, should be to give authors control over the integrity of their work and the right to be properly acknowledged and cited.

To say that this definition is widely accepted is not to say that it is entirely uncontroversial. For one thing, attentive readers will note that there is built into it an assumption that it applies only to peer-reviewed research literature, not to all scholarship in all disciplines, and yet OA in the humanities has been a growing phenomenon for years.[2] Nor do all OA advocates agree that unlimited reuse rights are an essential element of OA, or that the "only role for copyright in this domain should be to give authors control over the integrity of their work and the right to be properly acknowledged and cited."[3] We will discuss some of these issues in a bit more depth later in the chapter.

What is the difference between "open access" and "public access"?

Although not everyone agrees that OA necessarily includes unlimited reuse rights, those who do subscribe to that definition will often draw a distinction between open access (which grants to the public all of the rights that normally belong exclusively to the copyright holder), and "public access," a term used to describe access that is free but does not include the grant of all copyright prerogatives to the public.

This distinction came most prominently to public notice in the United States with the issuance of the White House Office of Science and Technology Policy's memo *Expanding Public Access to the Results of Federally Funded Research*.[4] This memo instructs every U.S. government agency that underwrites at least $100 million in research annually to "develop a plan to support increased public access to the results of research funded by the Federal Government." The memo was carefully written in terms of public access rather than open access, specifically because it requires only that the research results be made available to read and redistribute, not that the authors' copyright prerogatives be licensed to the public.

In connection with this policy directive, it is important to remember that while documents produced directly by government agencies and by government employees who are writing in their capacity as employees enter the public domain immediately and are not subject to copyright, the same is not true of documents that are produced by researchers and others whose work is supported by government grants, or who work for public universities. For copyright purposes, having one's independent scholarly or scientific work underwritten by government money does not make the published results of that work a "government document." If it did, then all government-funded research publications would automatically enter the public domain and the White House memo would have been unnecessary.

What are meant by "Green," "Gold," "Platinum," and "hybrid" OA?

These terms refer to the most common business models under which costs of publication may be recovered (and, in some cases, profit realized) in order to give the public free access.

The "Green" model is intended to serve as an overlay on the existing publishing system: Under this model, authors write and publish articles in traditional journals as they always have, but they deposit copies of their articles in institutional repositories (more on these later), which make them freely available to all. Very often, though not always, the version deposited is the author's final accepted manuscript rather than the final published version. It is also often the case that articles made available in this way are embargoed (i.e., their content made publicly inaccessible) for some period of time before being opened up to free access. This is usually to give the publisher a chance to sell access before access becomes free. (See below for a further discussion of why embargoes may be imposed and how they work.)

The "Gold" model is one that makes the final, published version of the article freely available, without any embargo period. In this case, the publisher's costs are usually covered either by some kind of institutional subsidy or by imposing on the author an article processing charge (APC). In this way, the publisher is relieved of having to recover costs by charging for access to the content, and is able to give it away for free. Generally speaking, the Gold model is understood to be underwritten by authors: The publisher's revenue comes from APCs that are levied on submitting authors, often (though not always) underwritten by grant funds. This is true of most Gold OA articles, but it is not the model used by the majority of Gold OA journals. (Don't worry, this will be explained later in the chapter.)

"Platinum" OA is an emerging term that is generally used to distinguish Gold OA that is based on institutional subsidy or some other kind of external funding, rather than on charging fees to authors. As of this writing, the use and application of this term is still somewhat unsettled and inconsistent.[5]

"Hybrid" is a term used to describe a model whereby the publisher provides authors the option of making their articles available on an OA basis within the context of what is otherwise a toll-access journal. If the author's paper is accepted, he has the option either to let it be published as usual and made available only to paying subscribers, or to pay an APC and make that article freely available. The term "hybrid" refers to the fact that when a journal takes this approach, the non-subscribing general public will experience each issue of the journal as a patchwork of free and toll-access content; typically, the OA articles are marked as such on each issue's table of contents page.

The hybrid model is controversial. The controversy arises chiefly from concern about "double dipping." Since the publisher continues to charge a subscription fee for full access to the journal, there is understandable suspicion in the scholarly world (and especially among OA advocates) that publishing a hybrid journal means getting paid twice, once by the author in return for the publishing service and then again by the subscriber in return for access to the article. This concern is compounded by the fact that in an online publishing environment, journals decreasingly have list prices; as noted above, the price for a subscription varies from customer to customer depending on local institutional characteristics. This makes it very difficult to tell whether or not the price of a hybrid title represents "double dipping" and leads to understandable suspicion on the part of its paying customers. While some publishers have made efforts to alleviate that suspicion, it is impossible to eliminate it entirely without making the company's book-keeping thoroughly transparent.

How does open access work across STM and HSS disciplines?

Given the differences in publishing practices and norms between these two broad categories of scholarship (for more explanation of which, see Chapter 9), it may not come as a surprise that issues of scholarly communication reform generally, and issues related to open access specifically, are viewed somewhat differently between those two worlds.

To some degree, this difference arises from the characteristics that separate the STM and HSS disciplines from each other: a relatively strong focus on strictly factual and often laboratory-based orientation in STM, and a greater prevalence of interpretive and inferential work among HSS scholars. Publications in the STM disciplines tend mainly to be oriented toward the factual reporting of clinical and laboratory findings or the presentation of logical proofs: What matters is not so much the way in which the ideas are expressed as the factual validity of the ideas themselves. A journal article that reports the findings of a laboratory experiment demonstrating the effectiveness of a flu vaccine, or laying out a proof that resolves a long-standing problem of mathematics, does not depend for its impact and effectiveness on the elegance of the language or the author's creative interpretation. To a significant degree, scientists publish in order to stake a claim: "I discovered X, and did so on Y date."

In the HSS disciplines, however, the author's interpretations and the way they are expressed will often be fundamental to the content of the article. An author who writes an argument for a novel reading of Walt Whitman's poetry, or who suggests previously unconsidered implications of social science data, is not presenting a newly discovered fact to the world but rather putting forward an argument that is to some degree debatable. In such a case, the way in which the argument is expressed is a fundamentally important part of the scholarship itself. Humanists, then, publish largely in order to propound arguments: "Here are some convincing reasons to believe that X is the case, or to take position A on issue B."

For these reasons (among others, including the predominance of public funding for research in the STM disciplines), the OA movement has been able to make much more headway in the sciences than in the humanities. Scientific authors tend to have more invested in establishing the priority of their findings and less invested in maintaining strict control over the *specific expression* of those findings; humanistic authors tend to have more invested in maintaining some degree of control over how their work is disseminated and reused.

Authors across all disciplines, of course, have (or would seem to have, at least) an interest in getting their ideas across to lots of people: A scientist who has staked a claim to a particular finding wants that claim widely recognized (partly as a hedge against counterclaims from others); a humanist who is arguing for a particular reading of the literature wants that argument to take hold among his colleagues and to influence them; a social scientist who believes we have misunderstood the data on preadolescent delinquency wants her argument to affect social policy. For this reason, OA advocates believe that the value propositions of OA—broadest possible readership, greater influence through wide reuse and adaptation—should be highly attractive across the board. But because scholarly and scientific authors publish for reasons other than simple dissemination, the cost/benefit balancing is more complex than that. After all, in the current information environment, *broad dissemination itself* is nearly cost-free for authors: If all one wishes to do is share one's work with the public, one may simply set up a free blog on which to post all of one's clinical findings and/or scholarly arguments. But as we discussed in Chapter 2, scholarly authors want—and, from a professional standpoint, need—more than just a dissemination service. In order for their work to be taken seriously by their colleagues, it must be certified as valid by well-informed and disinterested third parties. Scholarly and scientific authors in all disciplines place a great value on such certification, and the fact that they continue, in overwhelming numbers, to submit their work for publication in venues that restrict access to paying customers is a testament to the fact that certification generally matters to them more than the broadest possible dissemination does. This dynamic applies more or less equally in the STM and HSS disciplines.

What are the relative benefits and downsides of Green, Gold, and Platinum OA?

Like any publishing arrangement or program (including toll access), each of the various OA arrangements has a set of upsides and downsides.

The upsides of Green OA include the fact that it makes scholarly content freely available, and (where embargoes are imposed) it gives publishers at least a limited opportunity to sell access. (Not everyone will see the latter as an upside to the Green model, but some do.) On the downside, it very often involves delaying the public's access to the content, the version made freely available is often not the version of record, and to the degree that the content is offered immediately and in more-final versions, it poses a potential threat to the subscription model. (Not everyone will see the latter as a downside, but some do.)

The upsides of Gold OA include the fact that it makes scholarly content freely available in the versions of record and without delay. When it is funded by APCs, the biggest downside is the cost to the author—and those costs can be significant, sometimes in the thousands of dollars. Authors working in disciplines with a strong system of grant funding will often write APC costs into their grant proposals, anticipating that they will publish in a Gold OA journal. When this is the case, the chief downside of this model is the redirection of research funding away from new research and toward dissemination. Given the enormous budgets of funding agencies like the National Institutes of Health (in the United States) and the Wellcome Trust (in the United Kingdom), such policies can easily result in the redirection of hundreds of millions of dollars away from new research.

Platinum OA offers all of the benefits of Gold OA without creating new costs that authors must either cover themselves or find someone else to cover. The chief downside of the Platinum model is opportunity cost: If an institution is funding one or more OA journals, it is necessarily forgoing the other things that could have been done with that money. (However, since the same can be said of virtually any program or initiative undertaken by an organization, to cast this as a "downside" of Platinum OA itself, rather than simply a cost, may not be entirely fair. Everything an organization does costs money, and this is no more true of OA publishing than of any other initiative.)

What are "sponsored journals"? Are they like "predatory" journals?

Sponsored journals may or may not be deceptive, depending on whether they are open and above-board about their sponsorship. In either case, they are subject to a serious conflict of interest: If a pharmaceutical journal is sponsored by, for example, a drug company, then its sponsor has an interest in publishing studies that find its products to be safe and effective and in suppressing studies that find its products to be either unsafe or ineffective. Obviously, this interest conflicts with the journal's interest in publishing disinterested science.

The idea of a company paying for the creation and publication of a journal that purports to present disinterested science, while actually promoting that company's products, may seem bizarre, and unacceptable on its face. Such practices are indeed generally seen as unacceptable in the scholarly publishing world, but sadly they are not as unusual as one might think. Companies who engage in this kind of activity usually take steps to hide the fact that they are doing so, and sometimes they succeed for some time before they are discovered—but when they are, the scientific community's reaction is almost always swift and negative. For example, in 2009 it emerged that the pharmaceutical company Merck had paid Elsevier (a large commercial publisher of science journals) to publish a series of "journals" that consisted of previously published articles and article summaries that put Merck's products in a positive light.[6] Elsevier and Merck were pilloried in both the blogosphere and the professional literature—and rightly so.

Is it possible for a company to sponsor a journal in a way that is above-board and that will be seen as acceptable in the scholarly and scientific community? The answer is probably no, or at least a highly qualified yes. Advertising is certainly one widely accepted method of sponsorship, but it is controversial in the context of scholarly and scientific publishing. Beyond that, the general feeling in the community of scholarship and science is that there must be a high and impermeable wall between (on one side) the vetting and publication of research and (on the other) the promotion of commercial products. To allow a commercial enterprise—or even a nonprofit one—to underwrite the operation of a journal that presents itself as a publication of disinterested research is, ethically speaking, to play with fire.

The phenomenon of "predatory" journal publishing will be discussed in depth in Chapter 13.

What is an OA "megajournal"?

The megajournal is an ingenious invention of the OA community, one designed in order to take full advantage of the economies of scale afforded by the Internet, to encourage the publication of research that might otherwise be difficult to place in selective journals, and to make maximum amounts of high-quality scholarship and science freely available to the public.

Unlike a traditional journal (whether toll-access or OA), the megajournal does not reject submitted articles based on their lack of originality, anticipated low impact, or lack of novelty. The editors and peer reviewers of a megajournal focus exclusively on soundness of method: Does the author of a submitted paper demonstrate that the research design employed was rigorously established and provide evidence that sound laboratory methods were followed? Do the reported results follow clearly from the experimental design? If so, then the article is accepted, and it is left to readers to decide whether or not those results are worth their time to read and/or take into consideration as they plan related research in the future.

This model is ingenious in a number of ways. For one thing, it creates a path to publication for research results that otherwise would run into significant barriers: for example, studies designed to investigate the validity of earlier findings (by attempting to replicate them) or studies that result in null findings—both of which can be tremendously important. For selective journals, publishing such studies takes valuable space and editorial resources away from the presentation of new, startling, or controversial research. But because megajournals have effectively no space limitations and are invariably funded by APCs, this becomes a non-issue for them, and thus their emergence creates a new incentive for a much wider variety of useful research.

Megajournals are given that name because the publishing model they employ creates significant economies of scale, allowing them to publish thousands—and in some cases tens of thousands—of articles each year. Earlier in the chapter we noted that the majority of Gold OA journals do not charge APCs, but that the majority of Gold OA articles published each year *are* funded by APCs. The rise of megajournals is what explains this apparent paradox. A handful of APC-supported megajournals publish, together, tens of thousands of articles each year, whereas a much larger number of Gold OA journals publish many fewer articles without charging APCs. Thus, most Gold OA journals are not APC-supported, but most Gold OA articles are APC-supported.

Because OA megajournals are invariably funded by APCs, this model is also very attractive from a business perspective. As noted in Chapter 13, the APC funding model encourages acceptance of papers rather than rejection of them, and while that dynamic can (in the hands of the unscrupulous) result in the publication of garbage disguised as scholarship, it can also be used to underwrite the high-volume production of solid scholarly products.

How does OA apply to theses and dissertations?

Universities have generally kept copies of locally produced graduate theses and dissertations in their library collections. In the twentieth century, as space came to be more and more at a premium in research libraries (and in light of the relatively low levels of use seen by most theses and dissertations), libraries began sending dissertations out to third-party service providers for microfilming.

With the development of the Internet, online storage of theses and dissertations became increasingly attractive as a more cost-effective solution than microfilming, and one that makes those documents much more readily available to the public. Today, a growing number of academic institutions manage theses and dissertations on a fully electronic basis: The document is submitted and processed electronically and then archived online, often with a print copy held in a secure non-public space for archival purposes.

Putting theses and dissertations online has solved many problems (such as ease of access and the logistical problems of physical storage) but has created others—notably, issues around the potential downsides of making them freely and easily discoverable and readable by the general public. While this arrangement has obvious benefits, for doctoral candidates working in disciplines in which the publication of a first monograph is generally seen as an essential stepping-stone to an academic career, there have been concerns about whether making one's dissertation freely available will undermine the market for a formally published book based on that dissertation.

Here it is worth addressing a few of the vagaries of first-book publication in the humanities and social sciences. While it is true that publishing a scholarly monograph is a sine qua non of academic advancement in many humanistic disciplines, and while it is true that many young scholars' first books are based on their dissertations, it is also true that no reputable press is likely to publish a dissertation without extensive revision. It is not clear to what degree publishers care whether a book proposal is based on a publicly available dissertation, and this ambiguity is what can create anxiety among doctoral candidates preparing to enter the notoriously (and increasingly) cut-throat job market for humanist scholars. In response to that concern, many universities allow graduate students to place embargoes of two or three years on their online theses and dissertations, making the online versions unavailable to the public until the student has had time to shop the manuscript around to publishers.

Of course, to those who advocate for increased open access to scholarship, these concerns can seem paranoid and silly. Given the lack of compelling data showing that publishers care one way or another whether proposed books are based on publicly available dissertations, they see no reason for worrying about it so much. The tension between these two positions sometimes plays out in public, and can do so in fairly dramatic fashion. In 2013, for example, the American Historical Association issued a public statement calling on history departments to allow their doctoral students to embargo dissertations for up to six years (rather than the more traditional three) if they so choose, as long as they make print copies publicly available in their institutions' libraries immediately.[7] This proposal was met with significant protest from the OA community, and the controversy is ongoing.[8]

What is an institutional repository?

Institutional repositories (IRs), which are usually administered by academic libraries, serve two primary purposes.

First, they serve an archival function by storing and curating scholarly documents that are produced by the host institution. As mentioned above, it is increasingly common for university libraries to deposit electronic

copies of graduate theses and dissertations in their repositories rather than (or in addition to) keeping printed copies on the library shelves. In addition, faculty members are
usually invited to place copies of articles that they publish
in academic journals in the IR, where they can be certain
that the library will ensure the articles' preservation and
long-term availability. Many IRs offer space and curation
for scholarly products other than articles as well, including videos (such as of musical performances or art installa-
tions), conference posters, and research data sets.

Second, IRs serve a distribution function by making
the stored documents available to the world—usually
(though not always) without restriction on an OA basis.
Some IR platforms track usage data, allowing the library
to report back to the authors whose work is housed in the
IR on the number of downloads their work has received,
and even on where in the world the usage came from. It is
also increasingly common for libraries themselves to serve
as publishers of Platinum OA journals, using the IR as the
archive and content bed for articles. (This is discussed in
more detail in Chapter 6.)

It is important to note that when it comes to journal
articles, what are stored in an institutional repository are
very often not the versions of record. Some publishers
allow authors to make the version of record publicly available through a repository, while others only allow deposit
of the author's accepted manuscript. On the other side,
some funding agencies require that articles resulting from
research that they have funded be made publicly available in their versions of record, either immediately or after
some embargo period; others might only require that the
author's accepted manuscript be deposited. (For more discussion of the issue of versioning and the concept of "version of record," see Chapter 2.)

Is there such a thing as OA for books?

While, as noted above, the most widely accepted definitions of OA apply only to the peer-reviewed research literature, there is nothing stopping authors and publishers in humanities and other disciplines in which the book, rather than the journal article, is a central product of scholarship, from adopting OA principles to book publishing and characterizing the resulting programs as "open access." And, in fact, this has now been happening for some years and seems to be picking up speed and momentum as of this writing.

There have been several notable initiatives along these lines in recent years. One of them is Knowledge Unlatched (KU), which forges cooperative partnerships between traditional publishers, funding agencies, and libraries:[9] Publishers offer forthcoming books as candidates for "unlatching," participant libraries pledge an amount of money in support of the publication costs of the books, and if enough libraries pledge to support a book, it is published and made available for free (in pdf format) in perpetuity. As more libraries pledge, the cost per library goes down; thus, a library might pledge $40 in support of Book X, but what it ends up paying will be less than that if enough other libraries pledge as well. (Pledge amounts are capped, so the library will never be asked to pay more than what it has pledged.) The result is basically a crowd-funded e-book that is made freely available to all. Print copies and enhanced versions of the books may be made available for purchase as well, but the basic pdf version is available online on an OA basis.

Another important OA monograph project is a program called Luminos, which is run by the University of California Press.[10] Under this model, the author contributes about half the publication cost of the book (which UC

Press calculates as $15,000 on average, making the standard author fee $7,500), while the remainder of the cost is covered by a combination of the press, libraries that pay a membership fee, and revenue from print sales of the book. It is important to note that books are selected for publication under this program according to all of the same criteria as those that apply under their traditional publishing model, and authors are not required to participate in the Luminos program in order to have a book published by UC Press.

A very different model is used by Lever Press, an initiative that emerged from a cooperative partnership between the University of Michigan, Amherst College, and the Oberlin Group of liberal arts colleges.[11] Lever Press pools funds from all of its member institutions (which are generally libraries and are generally expected to redirect funds from their acquisitions budgets) to support the publication of OA monographs, rather than levying charges on authors or soliciting donations from outside the group. The resulting books are then made available on an OA basis. This not only allows the participants to make high-quality scholarly content available to the world at no charge, but also makes it possible for small colleges without university presses to become active producers of scholarly monographs. But in the case of Lever Press, monographs themselves are not ultimately the point—while the initial phases of the project are expected to be relatively book-centric, the group plans to expand its product line into new and different formats and manifestations of scholarship as well.

Book publishing poses a very different suite of challenges from the one that characterizes journal publishing, so we can likely expect to see more projects like these in the future and should expect them to vary quite widely in shape and content.

Does OA apply to research outputs other than traditional articles and books?

It can, and one area of particular interest and energy in recent years has been research data sets. The topic of "open data" is a locus of lively debate at the moment, and the shape of the debate is somewhat different from the one concerning open access to research publications, for a number of reasons.

For one thing—and this is centrally important—data are not generally subject to copyright. You cannot copyright a fact or an idea, only the *recorded expression* of a fact or an idea. For example, the fact that bears are mammals is not, itself, copyrightable. However, an author's original written explanation of what makes bears mammals is subject to copyright. One may write one's own explanation of the same general facts without infringing on that author's copyright, but simply repeating his explanation word for word in your own publication might well infringe on his copyright. (It also may constitute plagiarism; for more on how copyright and plagiarism intersect, see Chapter 5.)

When you get into compilations of facts that have been put together for a specific purpose, however—in short, data sets and databases—the copyright issue becomes a bit more murky. In copyright law there exists a provision for some degree of protection for compilations of facts or data, even if the individual components of those collections are not copyrightable in and of themselves, when the creation of the compilation involves a significant amount of effort and expense. But such provisions are not consistent from jurisdiction to jurisdiction. Ever since the *Feist* ruling in 1991, the United States has given little if any copyright protection to non-creative compilations of facts (such as phone numbers arranged alphabetically by residents' name).[12] In other countries, compilations of facts have greater or lesser protections under copyright law under what is generally known as the "sweat of the brow" doctrine, which holds that compilations of data should get some degree of copyright protection based on the investment of effort involved in creating them.[13]

In part because copyright law can be ambiguous when it comes to data sets, a branch of the OA movement is particularly concerned with encouraging the opening up of research data as a matter of policy. Just as research funders are increasingly requiring their grant recipients to give the public free and unrestricted access to the written results of their funded research, so too they are increasingly requiring that the underlying data be made freely available.

Making research data freely available—not only for examination, but also for reuse—provides at least two significant benefits to the public and to scholarship as a whole. First, it allows others to examine the data on which published research reports are based, making it easier for other scholars and scientists to see how the original researcher's conclusions were obtained. This can be enlightening and can also (perhaps more importantly) provide a check on sloppy or unscrupulous data interpretation. Second, it allows other researchers to reuse the data, either for replication purposes or in order to do entirely new research. The potential usefulness is tremendous.

However, open data initiatives carry with them significant costs as well as benefits. Data sets produced in some disciplines can be enormous—in the multiple terabytes, in some cases. The sheer costs of storage can be very high. And once the matter of storage is resolved, there remain the problems of data management and curation, which can be even more daunting in terms of logistics and expertise. Making data open requires more than robust archiving; it involves making the archived data findable and accessible. Findability requires metadata—coded descriptors that make the information discoverable by search engines and by people. And making the data accessible (once its existence has been determined) means the ongoing management of servers and networks. The more data you house, the greater the pressure on staff time and network integrity. As with published research, data openness is not only not free, it is not even close to being cheap. One important question, then, is how it will be paid for and who will do the paying. These are difficult questions that will have to be resolved over time, and the resolutions to them will probably vary by situation and context (and legal jurisdiction). And the solution or solutions upon which the scholarly and scientific community settles will invariably be controversial.

Should all scholarship be made available on an OA basis?

This is a question that causes a fair amount of controversy among members of the scholarly communication ecosystem. For many OA advocates, a world in which anyone is denied access to scholarly information based on an inability to pay for it is one in which the system has simply failed. From this binary point of view, there is a crisis in scholarly communication, and it is not a crisis of price—no matter how much or how little access to information costs, what matters is that there is a cost barrier between the information and the person who wants access to it. From this perspective, the goal of the OA movement should be to eliminate such barriers entirely. Others (who also consider themselves OA advocates) see no problem with, for example, nonprofit scholarly societies charging reasonable prices for access to the products they publish, since they use the revenues generated by those activities to further the scholarly work of their organizations. For those holding this view, OA should be about minimizing the costs of access to scholarly publications and the restrictions on reuse—but not about eliminating access costs entirely, since imposing those costs (within reason) can serve the purpose of furthering scholarship.

As mentioned above, there are also some who believe that OA is, by definition, a specific property of peer-reviewed scientific publications only, and that other kinds of academic publishing fall outside the sphere of OA by definition. For those who hold this position, it is taken as given that scholarly products of humanistic disciplines should be subject to different rules, partly because these products are much less likely to have been underwritten by significant public funding and partly because they tend to be, by their very nature, fundamentally interpretive and creative.

That last point is worth emphasizing. One of the arguments put forward by those who urge a different approach to OA in the humanities and social sciences than that widely promoted in the STM disciplines is that in the latter case, what matters most is not the expression of the facts, but the facts themselves. For example, when a publicly funded researcher discovers that a particular type of medical intervention is especially effective in treating malaria, that researcher's personal writing style is not a fundamentally important aspect of the resulting publication, nor is the purpose of the publication to give the researcher a forum for creative expression. However, if a professor of English literature formulates a significant new interpretation of a poem by T.S. Eliot and writes a book propounding that interpretation, the creative interpretation itself, and the ways in which that interpretation is expressed, are centrally important features of the scholarship. Making the English professor's work freely available for unfettered reuse has different implications for that professor's original work than doing the same for the malaria researcher's discovery. Should we make the former's work available on the same kind of OA basis as the latter's?

Like so many questions around access to scholarship, these are controversial and will likely remain so for some time.

13

PROBLEMS AND CONTROVERSIES IN SCHOLARLY COMMUNICATION

What is the "serials crisis"?

For the past several decades, librarians and other observers and participants in the scholarly communication ecosystem have been expressing alarm over the degree to which annual price increases for scholarly journals—especially those in the STM disciplines—tend to outstrip library budget growth. The prices of scholarly and scientific journals generally rise by 5% to 6% per year, with the averages for scientific journal prices trending higher and those for humanities titles rising a few points less, and significant differences between peer-reviewed and non–peer-reviewed journals as well.[1]

The impacts of this pricing dynamic have been complicated in recent years by the explosion in the number of journals available and by the emergence of publisher journal bundling (also known as the Big Deal, about which more below), which tends to drive down the unit cost of journal subscriptions while increasing the library's actual spend on journal content.[2] This complication has led to controversy about the reality and significance of the serials crisis, with some observers pointing out that libraries are actually spending less per journal article today than they once were, and that the budget pressure being felt by libraries is a result of an explosive growth in research output rather than an increase in unit cost.[3] One response from the library side is that while the unit cost of each article may not be rising, libraries are under increasing pressure to buy articles in bundles (whether at the journal or the package level), and the cost of those bundles is what continues to rise.[4]

Others have contended that the only reason library budgets fail to keep pace with journal price increases is that universities have been allocating less and less of their budgets to the library.[5] Still others have argued that it hardly makes sense to call a market dynamic a "crisis" when it has been known and dealt with for several decades—though this position leaves unanswered the question of what to do about the very real (and undisputed) gap between library budget trends and serial pricing trends, regardless of whether we characterize that dynamic as a "crisis."

Another factor that has compounded the controversy over journal prices is the fact that in the online environment, journal pricing has become both variable and opaque. During the print era, publishers generally charged a single price for each of their journals; an institutional subscription to the *Journal of the American Medical Association* cost the same whether your library served a large research university or a small liberal arts college. This reality largely reflected the fact that it cost the publisher no more to print and mail a physical issue to a large research university than it did to send that same issue to a small liberal arts college, and the fact that the publisher did not act as an ongoing provider of access to the journal's back issues— providing the services of archiving and ongoing access was the library's job.

With the migration of journal content online, however, two very important things changed: The publisher began providing online access to enormously different numbers of individuals from campus to campus, and the publisher (rather than the library) became the ongoing administrator of archived access to the subscribed content, buying and managing the servers on which those journal archives lived. Taking on the curation and management of online access certainly involved a new cost for publishers, a cost that one could reasonably expect to see reflected in higher pricing; the differential costs involved in serving larger and smaller campus populations are a bit more controversial. However, what selling online access has also allowed the journal publisher to do is set prices by thinking in terms of the product's value rather than the costs involved in creating it. For all of these reasons, among others, it is decreasingly the case that online journals have a set list price; instead, the library that is interested in a subscription contacts the publisher to ask for a quote, and the publisher sets a customized price for that library based, in significant part, on what it believes the library will be willing to pay in light of its budget, the size of the student population it serves, and local research and teaching needs.

Controversy will continue to rage over the reality, meaning, and future implications of the serials crisis. The questions that swirl around this topic will probably only begin being seriously answered when libraries start canceling subscriptions in significant numbers—an eventuality that is constantly predicted but somehow never quite materializes, at least partly because libraries have been reallocating money previously used for buying books to the preservation of journal subscriptions (more on this below). It is difficult to see how it can be avoided indefinitely, however.

Why are libraries buying fewer books?

Another aspect of the "serials crisis" that gets a bit less attention than the growing gap between journal prices and

library budgets, but one that is causing growing consterna-
tion among many members of the scholarly communication community, is actually an upshot of that dynamic: the
shift in library funding away from the purchase of scholarly
books. A study by ProQuest, published in early 2016, discovered two main trends with regard to library spending
on books. First, monograph budgets were getting smaller
in order to free up money to keep increasingly expensive
journal subscriptions going; second, e-books (rather than
print books) accounted for a growing share of the library's
remaining book expenditures.[6]

At least two major factors are contributing to these trends.

The first is that individual books are usually much
cheaper than journal or database subscriptions, which
means that it is much easier to respond positively to patron
requests for book purchases than to requests for new subscriptions. At most academic libraries, even ones with very
limited funding, the answer to a patron who says, "Would
you please buy this $75 book?" will be an automatic "yes."
By contrast, at most academic libraries (even ones with
relatively generous funding), when a patron asks, "Would
you please subscribe to this journal at a cost of $800 per
year?" the answer will be, "Let us get back to you on that."
In extreme cases of funding limitation, one might imagine a library simply no longer buying books at all except
in response to specific patron requests. (In Chapter 6 we
discuss patron-driven and demand-driven book-buying
models, which actually institutionalize purchasing along
these lines.) While it may seem, at first blush, as if the relative ease of book acquisition would lead to *more* books
being acquired by libraries in the face of rising journal subscriptions, what this reality actually means in practice is
that libraries are increasingly free to forgo buying books
on a proactive and predictive basis and instead wait for
demand to be demonstrated.

Second—and more controversially—journal content tends to be used much more heavily than books are, and especially more so than scholarly books. Not only do journals get heavier use, but the circulation of books in research libraries has been declining rapidly over the past twenty years in absolute terms.[7] This observation is controversial partly because the trend is not universal; there are research libraries (though not many) in which this is not happening, and the reality is more complicated in liberal arts colleges and comprehensives. It is also controversial because it is so troubling; librarians hate to think that students are using books less, and many librarians and scholars worry about the implications of declining book use for the future of university presses and of authors writing in specialized areas of scholarship. And yet the trend seems to be undeniable and it is not clear what can (or should) be done to reverse it.

What is the "Big Deal" and why is it a big deal?

Journal publishing has not yet, and may never, move completely out of the print and into the online realm. However, scholarly journal publishing is now an overwhelmingly online enterprise, and this shift has had far-reaching impacts on editorial processes and access models. One of the most disruptive of these impacts has come with the emergence of publisher journal packages, also known (often derisively) as the Big Deal.

The way a Big Deal typically works is that a publisher will approach a library with an offer along the following lines. Suppose the company publishes 100 journals, the total cost of which would be $100,000 if a library subscribed to them all individually, and suppose that this particular library subscribes to 40 of those and is paying $40,000 per year for them. The publisher (recognizing that it could grant the library's users access to its entire catalog of online journals at little additional cost to itself) offers the library access to the entirety of its journal list at a very advantageous marginal increase in price—say, an additional $20,000 for access to the entire catalog. If accepted, this deal means that the library will now be paying $60,000 for access to $100,000 worth of journals.

Typically, however, there is a catch: If the library accepts this offer, it must agree not to subsequently cancel any of the subscriptions from its original list (thereby sneakily securing access to the entire catalog of 100 journals for only $20,000). Thus, libraries that enter into these agreements realize significant benefits (access to a large amount of new journal content at a very low per-journal price) but also enter into an agreement that imposes significant restrictions (the inability to pick and choose from that publisher's offerings, or to reduce the amount of money it spends on that publisher's journals). Compounding the problem is the fact that the price one pays for the Big Deal is determined significantly by the amount of content one was already buying from the publisher at the time the Big Deal was offered—so a library that subscribed to only 10 of our hypothetical publisher's 100 titles will likely realize a much larger marginal benefit from the Big Deal than will one that previously subscribed to 40 of them. It is never easy to say for certain whether this is the case, however, since the pricing of such packages is invariably kept under wraps and protected by confidentiality agreements.

The term "Big Deal" seems to have been invented by Kenneth Frazier in an article titled "The Librarians' Dilemma: Contemplating the Costs of the 'Big Deal.'"[8] In his discussion, Frazier lays out a number of the challenges associated with this model, comparing the situation it creates to the Prisoner's Dilemma, in which "individually rational action results in persons being made worse off in terms of their own self-interested purposes." The deal is tremendously attractive and truly does, in many cases, provide outstanding short-term value in terms of cost per article; however, by binding itself to a constant annual increase in a larger amount of spending for one particular publisher's content, the library locks itself into an arrangement that, over time, commits more and more of the library's budget to that one publisher's products and leaves less and less money to spend on anything else (such as, for example, books).

There are other reasons for libraries to be concerned about the Big Deal. For one thing, the less likelihood there is of a journal subscription being canceled by library customers, the less incentive there is for the publisher to maintain that journal's quality—and the more that customers are locked into Big Deals, the more that problem grows. Furthermore, some librarians have expressed concern that publishers are actually creating new, low-quality journals in order to pad their title lists and make their Big Deals look like bigger and better deals than they really are—though this is a difficult hypothesis to prove.

And this is why the Big Deal is such a big deal. For libraries and publishers both, the stakes are quite high. In some research libraries, Big Deals account for hundreds of thousands of dollars per year, and even more in some larger and more richly funded libraries. The cost is very high, it grows inexorably from year to year, and it almost invariably grows at a rate much higher than the rate of annual increase for any library budget. This means that every year the library must buy less of something else in order to keep paying for the Big Deal. But there is no way to decrease one's spending on the Big Deal without canceling it wholesale—and in many cases, doing so would be deeply painful for the faculty and students who have come to rely on access to the journals involved, and in some cases it would actually cost the library more to break up the Big Deal and subscribe only to the most heavily used titles than it does to simply keep paying for the Big Deal. This is a real quandary that has many librarians (and even some publishers) losing sleep. It is difficult to see what a solution to this problem would look like unless that solution is the complete upending of our current scholarly communication system and its replacement by something radically different—a possibility that will be discussed later in the book.

Which is better—printed books or e-books?

As one might expect, the answer to this question is not straightforward. The only possible answer is "it depends," and what it depends on varies based on one's perspective and on the role of books in one's work as a reader, a publisher, a library, or a researcher. We will look at a few of the pros and cons of e-books and print books from each of those perspectives.

Publishers

For publishers, the printed book poses a number of serious challenges. For one thing, physical books are usually produced in print runs: The publisher tries to anticipate how many copies will sell and prints a number close to that figure. Invariably, that figure is wrong: Either the run sells out (in which case the publisher has to decide whether to print more), or it does not sell out (in which case the publisher is left with remainders, which have to be discarded or sold at a steep discount). Another challenge is the sheer cost of printing, warehousing, and shipping.

Both of these challenges are obviated by the e-book format, which does not require the production of print runs, shipping, or physical warehousing. However, the e-book format poses its own challenges. For one thing, there is not a single standard e-book format; there are many, and publishers have to make difficult choices about how to present their e-book products. For another thing, the creation of e-books requires a whole new set of skills and different kinds of capital equipment, all of which cost money to establish and then to maintain—which the publisher must do while continuing to provide printed books as well. The challenges of archiving and curation are significant as well, and in the e-book realm publishers tend to be expected to take those challenges on with regard to their own publications (while allowing others, notably libraries, to perform that function as well).

Libraries

If anything, libraries have been even more ambivalent about e-books than publishers are—even as they have begun buying them in large quantities. The library profession has, for centuries, been fundamentally identified as caretakers of printed books, and library buildings have been designed for that express purpose. This means, among other things, that for libraries the shift from printed to online materials has required a significant rethinking of both day-to-day workflows and, to some degree, the deeper purposes of the profession. It is also true that e-books pose special challenges for libraries because they act like subscriptions rather than like outright purchases: When the library "buys" an e-book, it is usually purchasing a more or less permanent right of access to content held and maintained elsewhere, rather than a physical object or electronic file over which the library has local control. On the other hand, e-books provide the library an unparalleled opportunity to provide patrons with access wherever they are, to allow more than one patron to use the book at a time, and to provide full-text searchability of books, none of which is possible in the print realm. E-books can also be purchased by libraries in large bundles, which tend to provide an outstanding value (as measured in cost per title) but also create significant inefficiencies (in that the bundle invariably contains both wanted and unwanted content). E-books also make possible demand-driven acquisition (see Chapter 6 for more discussion of this concept), which itself evokes deeply ambivalent reactions among librarians.

Researchers

In this context we will define a "researcher" as someone who needs to interrogate the content of a book rather than read it from beginning to end—in other words, as distinct from a "reader," about whom more below. The researcher wants to find discrete pieces of information within the body of the text and therefore treats the book more as a database of content than as a linear and immersive reading experience. (It should be clear that reading and researching are not mutually exclusive, that they are both valid and worthwhile approaches to take with a book, and that one approach may be more or less appropriate than the other depending on context.) For researchers, e-books tend to offer mostly upsides rather than downsides. The two major advantages of the e-book format to researchers are its searchability and its portability. Rather than depending on an index (which may or may not be granular enough to suit the researcher's purpose, and may or may not define concepts in the way a particular researcher would), the researcher can search the entire text of the book looking for individual words or phrases. In most cases, this represents a huge advantage over the printed book. And the portability of e-books is also an enormous plus: An academic with access to her library's collection of online books will have that access wherever she is in the world, provided she has Internet access.

Readers

For readers—those who wish to engage the text of a book in an immersive, linear, and extended way—e-books pose perhaps the most thorny assortment of upsides and downsides. On the one hand, advances in e-book reader technology have made on-screen reading much more comfortable than it has ever been, and the portability aspect of e-books is also important in this context. When it comes to portability, a Kindle e-book reader is not much more convenient than a printed book, but it is dramatically more convenient than fifty printed books, and thus the Kindle (along with its competitor devices) is a huge boon to the business traveler, the cruise ship passenger, and the bus commuter. Consumer e-books are also usually cheaper than printed books, and they take up no shelf space in the home. On the other hand, for many people there is a visceral, sensual pleasure to the reading of printed books: the feel of the binding, the smell of the paper, the turning of the pages. These things are lost with e-books. And, of course, the battery does not run out on a printed book (though printed books are much harder to read in the dark).

What all of these competing pros and cons add up to is a complicated reality that shows no signs of simplifying. E-books and printed books are locked in a somewhat uncomfortable coexistence, each of them meeting different needs for different people in different reading and research contexts, which means that although e-books are clearly here to stay, they are not likely to drive the printed book to extinction anytime soon.

Why is peer review controversial?

As discussed in Chapter 4, peer-reviewed publication has long been the gold standard of scholarly publishing in most academic disciplines. A peer-reviewed journal is one that subjects submitted articles not only to the oversight and review of an editor, but also to the scrutiny of one or more other scholars in the author's field who assess the article's relevance and significance and the quality of its methodology and argumentation, and who then recommend publication, revision, or rejection. Authors want to publish in peer-reviewed journals because doing so signals to their peers that their work is of the highest quality, and peer-reviewed publication is very often essential to gaining and keeping employment on an academic faculty.

But does it work? Does peer review actually ensure that the resulting publications are, in fact, of high quality?

The answer, of course, is "it depends." For one thing, not all journals that promise rigorous peer review provide it. While relatively few simply lie about doing peer review, some manage the process very poorly, leaving papers in limbo for months or longer. There are also peer reviewers who agree to provide rigorous analysis but in fact give their assigned papers only cursory review. Some of the journals and publishers that engage in shoddy or nonexistent peer review are trying to do it well but failing; others, unfortunately, do actively misrepresent their processes (more on the problem of deceptive journal publishing practices below).

All of the discussion above has been about peer review in academic journals, but it is worth pointing out again that scholarly monographs are very often subjected to a form of peer review prior to publication as well.

There is a related question here as well: Does a paper or book have to be peer-reviewed in order for it to represent high-quality scholarship or trustworthy science? The answer to this question is obviously no; peer review tends to be valued by scholars and readers not because it is a fail-safe guarantor of quality, nor because it is the *only* way to guarantee quality, but rather because it is a system that they believe generally works well—or, at least, better than most other alternative systems.

How (if at all) should we measure the impact of scholarly publications?

The concept of measuring not just the *quality* but also the actual *impact* of journal articles is an increasingly controversial one.

The difference between quality and impact is an important one that bears explanation. *Quality* speaks to the intrinsic merits of a piece of scholarship: Is its argument sound, is it well written, does the research methodology follow accepted scientific norms, do the conclusions follow from the data, and so forth? Assessments of quality are usually made prior to publication by a journal or book publisher's editorial staff. Indeed, the whole purpose of an editorial staff, including peer reviewers, is to ensure that the publisher or journal selects high-quality work that is relevant to the target audience. (Relevance, or scope, is a particularly important criterion, of course: A chemistry journal is unlikely to publish a scholarly article on comparative linguistics, no matter how good the article is.)

Impact is a very different matter. When we measure the impact of a journal, we are trying to figure out whether and to what degree it has had an effect on the thinking and publishing taking place elsewhere within its field. A publication may be of very high quality and yet have little actual impact (if, for example, it deals with a subject area so abstruse that no one reads it).

The problem with impact is that you have to measure it, and measuring impact is difficult. One problem with measuring impact is that the traditional tools available for doing so tend to focus on the journal, not on individual articles. It is journals, not articles, that are given impact factors. This is another area in which the altmetrics movement seeks to create change.

Another problem with measuring impact arises from the difference between impact and quality mentioned above, and the fact that "impact" is a value-neutral measure. A truly terrible article may have a tremendous impact on the profession as measured by citations (all of them being examples of other authors citing it as an example of ludicrous idiocy) but have no substantive impact at all on the development of the discipline itself.

Issues surrounding the measurement of impact and other parameters of scholarly publishing are discussed further in Chapter 10.

Do scholarly and scientific journals accept advertising? Should they?

Many scholarly journals do not accept advertising and rely for their support on access fees paid (in the form of subscriptions) by readers or libraries. However, many other journals do accept advertising, and these may be found across subject areas and disciplines. For example, *Notes* (the quarterly journal of the Music Library Association) features a section of full- and half-page advertisements at the end of every issue. The advertisers are music publishers, vendors, and other commercial firms whose products are reviewed in the journal. In the sciences, journals like *Nature*, the *British Medical Journal*, and the *Journal of Chemical Education* all accept advertising.

How do scholarly and scientific publications manage the conflicts of interest that arise when they accept advertising money from companies whose products are being evaluated or otherwise reported on in those publications' pages?

The answer is that they do it with varying degrees of scrupulousness and success. In journalism, there has long been a tradition of what is commonly called "the separation of church and state." In this formulation, the "church" is the publication's editorial side (which decides what will be published and oversees the writing of what is published), and the "state" is the advertising side (which decides what advertisements will be accepted and how much advertisers will be charged). The idea has always been that these two areas of the publishing enterprise should operate independently of each other and that the organization should be especially careful not to let the "state" side influence the "church" side. In other words, if the journal's editors are reviewing an article based on a study that demonstrates the medical dangers of cigarette smoking, the advertising department should not be able to quash that article in order to curry favor with a potentially high-paying advertiser from the tobacco industry.

As one might imagine, this is (and has always been) an imperfect system, and publications have always had mixed success in maintaining the church/state division.

What is "predatory publishing"?

The rise of the Internet has brought radical change to many aspects of publishing generally, and of scholarly communication in particular. One of those changes has been a dramatic lowering of the barriers of entry to publishing. In the print era, it was not easy to become a publisher: To do so meant not only organizing and implementing editorial and review processes, but also purchasing capital equipment and establishing expensive relationships with printers and distributors. Both editing and copyediting required specialized skill, and one's publication had to be designed, laid out, and typeset. With the development and wide availability of free and simple tools for creating homemade Web pages, it has become relatively cheap and easy to create an online publication—and, unfortunately, it is now both cheap and quite easy to create an online entity that has the look and feel of a legitimate scholarly publication, even if it is in fact nothing more than a clearinghouse for whatever shoddy scholarship (or even outright nonsense) one wishes to place in it.

What motivation might one have to do so, though? How could one make money by offering a bad product, even if it costs relatively little to bring it to market?

In order to answer this question, we must back up and examine one of the defining complexities of the scholarly communication ecosystem: the fact that publishers are selling different products and services to different members of the scholarly community. To readers (or those, like libraries, who broker access on behalf of readers) publishers sell a product—like books or journals—in return for money. To authors they sell the services of publication in return for the right to sell access to the authors' work. Readers and libraries trade money for access, while authors trade publication rights for publishing services.

However, the Internet makes it easy to implement a different sort of business model, one that turns the traditional access-and-service model around by *selling* publication services to authors and *giving away* the resulting published content freely to readers. To be sure, "vanity publishing"—a system whereby a company publishes whatever an author wants to have published, regardless of its quality, and makes its money by charging the author directly for the publishing service—has existed for many years. However, "predatory" publishing is not the same thing as vanity publishing. The biggest difference between vanity and predatory publishing lies in the centrality of *deception* to the business model in the latter case. In other words, vanity publishing does not typically pretend to be anything other than what it is: a way for authors to bypass the traditional filter of editorial review and simply make their work available to the public without having to worry about whether someone else thinks it is worth publishing (we will discuss this further below). Predatory publishers, however, are in the business of deceiving. They may try to trick authors into believing their work is being published in a prestigious (or at least legitimate) venue, or readers into believing that they are reading rigorously vetted scholarship. Or, perhaps most perniciously, they may exist for the purpose of helping unscrupulous authors to trick their peers and colleagues into believing their work has been given the imprimatur of publication in a legitimate journal, when in fact it was accepted for publication simply because the author was willing to pay the necessary fee.

The term "predatory publishing" was coined by Jeffrey Beall, a librarian at the University of Colorado, Denver, who created a website titled *Scholarly Open Access: Critical Analysis of Scholarly Open-access Publishing* in 2008 (now defunct, but archived online).[9] On that site he listed publishers that, in his judgment, were "potential, possible, or probable" predators. The criteria he used for selecting publishers for his list included the following:

- Whether or not they seem to abide by such broadly accepted standards of publishing behavior as those promulgated by the Open Access Scholarly Publishers Association, the Committee on Publication Ethics, and the International Association of Scientific, Technical & Medical Publishers

- Whether the same editorial board is listed for multiple journals
- Whether the publisher hides its true center of operations
- Whether the publisher's journals seem designed to deceive either readers or authors regarding institutional affiliation
- Whether the publisher solicits contribution by means of mass e-mail messaging.

Beall's List (as it was informally known) was controversial for a number of reasons. For one thing (and least surprisingly), it attracted the anger of publishers featured on the list, some of whom threatened him with legal action.[10] However, it was also controversial because it defined predatory publishing specifically as a characteristic of open access (OA) journals. This left Beall susceptible to charges that his criticism of predatory publishers masked what was really an antagonism toward OA generally, and that if it were not for that antagonism, he would have broadened his conception of "predation" to include the behaviors of toll-access publishers that engage in unsavory practices that could reasonably be labeled "predatory" (such as exploiting their monopoly power to raise prices unfairly, buying low-priced society journals and raising their prices dramatically, etc.).

The topic of OA publishing was discussed in detail in Chapter 12, but here it is worth mentioning again that one model of OA publishing does involve author-side payments that provide the publisher with its revenue and allow the published article to be made freely available to readers. While the world of toll-access publishing also features limited author-side charges (often called "page charges"), particularly in certain science fields, these are very different from author-subsidized OA publishing because these charges do not replace access fees; instead, they supplement them or help the publisher to keep access fees lower. Because these publishers still rely for their revenue streams on readers being pleased with the quality of the articles they publish, page charges in a toll-access journal do not create the same conflict of interest as that created when a journal relies entirely on author-side fees for its revenue stream.

OA journals that rely on article processing charges (APCs) do find themselves unavoidably in a conflict of interest, because their financial interest is served entirely by accepting papers, and rejecting papers goes against their financial interest. In other words, relying on APCs puts their interest in fiscal viability in conflict with their interest in acting as arbiters of scientific and scholarly quality—which necessarily means publishing good papers and rejecting poor ones, not accepting as many papers as possible. This means that while predatory publishing is not technically a characteristic of OA publishing itself, it will inevitably be a problem for any segment of the publishing marketplace that provides content freely to readers while relying on APCs for its revenue stream. This does describe a significant segment of the OA publishing world, and it does not describe any significant part of the toll-access publishing world.

However, since the term "predatory" is quite subjective and could reasonably be applied to any number of unscrupulous or unethical practices that have nothing to do with specific revenue models, the controversy over that designation does suggest that the term itself may be too vague to be useful, and at least one industry observer has suggested that in the case of "predatory" OA journals, a term like "deceptive" might be both more accurate and more useful.[11]

How do you identify a predatory publisher?

With some difficulty, because (for obvious reasons) they typically try very hard to hide what they are doing. When trying to determine whether a publisher is legitimate or not, we look for behaviors like the following:

- Promising rigorous peer review, but in fact accepting for publication any submission that is accompanied by the required APC
- Claiming editorial board members who have not agreed to serve
- Publishing articles that have no relevance to the stated disciplinary field of the journal
- Claiming an organizational address in a prestigious location, when the publisher's base of operations is really elsewhere
- Claiming a high impact factor, when the journal in fact has no impact factor at all
- Fashioning the journal title in a way designed to suggest connection with a prestigious organization (which may or may not exist)
- Sending messages indiscriminately to hundreds (or thousands) of scholars and scientists, soliciting papers for publication—even if the authors' fields of research have nothing to do with the stated scope of the journal

Because predatory publishers very often create products that are of transparently poor quality and obviously sub-par scholarship, one might well ask why they are able to stay in business. And in fact, very often they do go out of business quickly—but since it is very cheap and easy to create a website that has all the superficial trappings of a

legitimate publisher, when a predator is caught and identified, it can be the work of less than a day for its operator
to take down the original website and open another with
a completely different name, a new fictitious address, a
new list giving the names of a fake editorial board, and
so forth—and, of course, immediately begin soliciting new
contributions from authors.

But this begs another question: Why would authors
contribute content to predatory publications? The answer
lies in the fact that predatory publishers target two primary categories of victim with their scams: (1) authors and
(2) authors' readers and their colleagues.

The first category of target for a predatory publisher
is authors themselves. The idea is that authors who need
formal and prestigious publication in order to secure their
careers, believing that they will receive genuinely credible
and rigorous publishing services, will submit their articles
to the predatory journal without investigating too closely
the journal's bona fides. The problem with this business
model is that while it is easy to set up a superficially
legitimate-looking journal website, it is not so easy to set
up an illegitimate journal website that will pass scrutiny
on the part of authors who genuinely care about publishing in legitimate and well-regarded journals.

This brings us to the second category of victim targeted
by predatory publishers: authors' readers and colleagues.
While a close look at its website will usually reveal very
quickly the scam nature of a predatory journal, the target
of its scam is not always the aspiring author. On the contrary, in many cases of predatory publishing the author is
complicit with the publisher in presenting scholarly garbage as if it were gold. The arrangement works this way:
An author is in need of two or three peer-reviewed publications to beef up his curriculum vitae before going up
for tenure review, but time is short: The review is in two

months, and he knows that for the better journals in his disciplines, the typical time lag between submission and publication can be six months or more—and that is assuming the paper gets accepted. But the author remembers getting an e-mail from another journal, one he has not heard of before, but which publishes in his field (or at least one closely related) and promises rigorous peer review, solid editorial support, and publication within two weeks of acceptance. Even better, the journal claims a high impact factor. The author pays a submission fee that might amount to anywhere from $75 to $2,000, submits his paper, quickly receives a positive response, and one month later has a new citation for his CV. (In the meantime, he has submitted two other articles to different journals from the same publisher, with the same results in each case.)

In a scenario like the one described above, should the author be suspicious? Of course. But if the author is more interested in making his CV look better than in securing genuinely rigorous review and editorial services, and if there are significant rewards at stake in making his CV look better, then he will be incentivized not to look too closely at the legitimacy of his publishing forum. And when all is said and done, his three publications in scam journals will be nestled on his CV alongside publications in legitimate journals—and there will be no obvious difference between the two categories of citation. While the website of a predatory journal may be revealingly amateurish and crude, a citation to that journal will look just like the citation to a real one. Authors who attempt to deceive their colleagues in this way do, of course, run the risk that someone will look up all the publications in their CVs and discover their deception—but in many cases, the risk of exposure is relatively low and may be outweighed by the great benefits conveyed by the appearance of scholarly achievement.

Do "predators" of this kind operate in scholarly contexts other than publishing?

Yes. In addition to publishing, predatory actors in the scholarly marketplace also operate in the realm of conferences and meetings. The scam is perpetrated along roughly the same lines as the one involved in predatory publishing. Potential contributors are invited to submit papers for presentation at the conference, and (surprise!) their papers are invariably accepted. In return for the payment of one or more fees, they are invited to present their papers and thus add a legitimate-sounding entry to their CVs. The conference will typically claim a list of prestigious names for its review board (many or most of whom are not actually associated with the conference) and will also claim that the presentation proposals will be rigorously vetted, implying that only the best will be accepted. The conference might also take place in an exciting locale so as to make the invitation that much more attractive. In reality, of course, the conference accepts all submitted proposals. The end result is that the conference organizers make lots of money, and the presenters end up with legitimate-looking additions to their CVs (and perhaps an enjoyable trip to a fun locale, paid for by their institutions or by grant funds).

It is worth noting that predatory journals do sometimes publish high-quality research content. The problem with these journals is not that they publish only garbage; the problem with them is that they lie about the services they offer, they help unscrupulous authors deceive their colleagues and institutions, they undermine the reputation of scholarly publishing, and they hurt the reputation of open access. This brings us to our next question.

What is the difference between predatory publishing and vanity or subsidy publishing?

Predatory publishing does share some important characteristics with subsidy publishing (also known more pejoratively as "vanity" publishing), but there are important differences. Subsidy publishing is mainly a property of the book world, and the bread and butter of this industry is the author who either has not been able to get her book placed with a traditional publisher, or who knows that the book is not marketable and simply wants to have it bound and printed in copies sufficient for some kind of personal use. (Imagine, for example, a family history produced by one member of a large and extended family, who then pays to have it printed and bound in enough copies that it can be distributed to all family members.) An author might also use a subsidy publisher in order to publish a book that she intends to try to market and sell herself, or a book on a topic about which she is passionate but for which she knows there to be a very narrow and limited audience (too narrow and limited to be worth pitching to a conventional publisher). What is very important to bear in mind is that there is nothing wrong with subsidy publishing—and no stigma attached to it—when it is carried out in an honest and above-board way.

There have, however, been examples in the scholarly world of publishing enterprises that occupy a murky middle ground between legitimate subsidy publishing and deceptive or predatory publishing. Since these publishers are invariably in the business of selling the books that result from their activities (rather than providing them freely on an OA basis), this issue is discussed more fully in Chapter 7.

14

THE FUTURE OF SCHOLARLY COMMUNICATION

The obvious question for us to address in this final chapter is a deceptively simple-sounding one: *What will the future of scholarly communication look like?* But we should probably break that question into more manageable chunks.

What will scholarly journals look like in the future?

This question is a good place to start, because journal publication is centrally important across virtually all scholarly disciplines. Even in the humanities, where tenure decisions often hinge on the publication of scholarly monographs, placing articles in prestigious peer-reviewed journals is also fundamentally important.

By now it is clear that open access (OA) has become, and is going to remain, an important and fairly pervasive feature of the journal publishing landscape. It is not evenly distributed and may never be, given the very different economic and professional dynamics across disciplines and scholarly cultures; however, the future will undoubtedly see a growing number of fully OA and hybrid OA journals. At this point it seems fairly certain that the market share of OA is going to stop somewhere short of 100%, but how far short remains an open question.

A more fundamental question concerns the future of the journal itself as a platform for the formal publication of research results. And this is a question with (at least) two parts: One has to do with the journal as an entity, and the other with the journal *issue* as a format.

As for the journal as an entity: As mentioned in Chapters 2 and 4, the journal itself serves a very important role as a branding mechanism for scholarly work. In the Internet era, formal publication in a journal is no longer necessary for those who simply want to make their work available to readers. In fact, if one's goal is to make one's work available to the maximum number of readers, then publication in a formal journal that charges readers for access to its content is, at least to some degree, self-defeating. But scholarly and scientific authors generally want more than just to make their work available—they want their work to be branded with the imprimatur of a journal that is known for presenting rigorous and high-quality content, and they want their work to be actively marketed to their peers. Getting one's work published in highly selective and high-reputation journals is absolutely key to job security and advancement in many academic disciplines. This means that regardless of what happens with access models and new modes of publication, there is a strong likelihood that the idea of the *journal as a branding entity* will persist for the foreseeable future.

What is much less obvious is what kind of future the idea of the *journal issue* has. Consider the fact that the journal issue represents an artificial bundling of content and the issuing of that content on a periodic basis (usually monthly or quarterly). This was a practice that made good sense in the print era, when the alternative—sending out articles individually as they were made ready for publication—would have been cost-prohibitive. It makes far less sense in an online information environment, one in which the artificial nature of a monthly or quarterly issue becomes painfully apparent: When an article is ready, why wait to publish it online? And in fact, already we see journal publishers moving away from this model, and instead publishing their journals as a more or less steady stream of online articles rather than in bundles. It seems clear that while the journal itself still has a long life ahead of it, the concept of the journal issue is already fading in importance.

In Chapter 12, we made note of the emergence of "megajournals," which publish much greater quantities of content than toll-access journals do, and which accept submissions based purely on what the editors and peer reviewers judge to be sound scientific practice (rather than the novelty or likely impact of the research). This model is growing in popularity, in part because it represents a highly profitable business model, and it seems likely to turn into a permanent part of the scholarly communication landscape. Successful megajournals like *PLOS ONE*, *Nature Communications*, and *Scientific Reports* currently publish thousands and even tens of thousands of articles per year and show no signs of going away. The constant growth in research output around the world (and thus the constantly growing number of authors needing a prestigious publishing venue for their work) strongly suggests that the scholarly publishing landscape will feature an increase in the number of megajournals over time.

What is the future of the scholarly monograph?

Our response to this question must be a bit more guarded. One can hardly imagine a more widely respected category of scholarly document; to say that one has published a monograph-length study is to achieve instantly a certain level of respect in any social gathering of academics, and as noted earlier in this book, the publication of a monograph with a university press is a requirement for tenure in many academic disciplines in the humanities and social sciences. The monograph format—with its potential for sprawling length and its ability to accommodate careful and extensive annotation—is generally seen as essential to the development of extended and complex scholarly arguments. This means that two important factors—continued prestige and the continued need on the part of authors to write and publish them—are contributing to the sustained vitality of the monograph.

Unfortunately, however, a third factor is necessary for the monograph to survive, and that factor is demand. In this regard, developments in recent years have not been particularly kind to the monograph. As noted in Chapter 6, the use of printed books in research universities' libraries has been declining both steadily and precipitously for more than a decade (although that trend is less strong in the libraries of liberal arts colleges), while demand for access to scholarly and scientific journal articles has remained very strong and the number of journals has grown explosively. The combination of (on the one hand) strong ongoing demand for journal content, steady growth in the amount of journal content available, and quickly rising journal prices and (on the other hand) stagnating or falling demand for monographs has severely undermined the library market for scholarly book publishing. In order to keep up with demand for journal content, many research libraries are simply shifting funds away from book purchasing in order to shore up subscriptions.

Another complicating factor for the monograph has been the nearly wholesale shift of scholarly communication from a print-based environment to a digital and networked one. The online world is a particularly hospitable place for journal articles, which are relatively short and convey the findings of narrow and focused studies. Most articles can easily and comfortably be read online on computer screens or devices (or quickly and conveniently printed up for offline reading), and scholarly journal publishing had begun moving quickly and decisively onto the Internet before the end of the 1990s. The Internet is a much less comfortable environment for the consumption of monographs, however. While novels and popular nonfiction are well served by various kinds of e-book devices designed to facilitate extended reading, scholarly work is more likely to take place on desktop and laptop computers, the displays of which are less amenable to the extended and linear design that is part and parcel of the monograph format. This fact, among others, has kept the scholarly monograph from moving as quickly into the online realm as the journal did. While it can increasingly be taken as given that a new university press publication will be made available in both print and e-book formats (though perhaps not simultaneously), it has taken much longer for this to become the case than many in the scholarly communication ecosystem expected it to.

Here it is perhaps worth pointing out that the Internet is by no means a wholly hostile environment for books. In Chapter 7, we touched briefly on the fact that a very common use case for scholarly monographs is not one that involves extended linear reading at all, but rather one that involves using the book as a database—as a store of information that the reader interrogates rather than reads, looking for particular and discrete pieces of information. (Anyone who ever emerged from the library stacks with ten books on a topic, intended to use them as sources for a five-page research paper, will immediately recognize this "reading" scenario.) One of the great advantages of the

e-book is that, unlike a printed book, it can be used effectively as a database. The only effective way to "search"
the full text of a printed book is by reading it—and while
reading a book is certainly a praiseworthy activity, in
many contexts it is not the best way to find out what information the book contains. (Would it make sense to read
ten monographs cover to cover in the course of writing
a five-page research paper?) While printed monographs
do often have indexes designed to guide the researcher
to particular pieces of information, an index provides
only a crude and schematic roadmap to the book's content, whereas full-text searching provides comprehensive
access to it.

On balance, however, it is not clear that the general
direction in which the scholarly communication ecosystem
is moving is going to be a healthy one for the monograph.
While no one expects the scholarly monograph to become
extinct in the foreseeable future, it seems likely that its
commercial prospects will continue to narrow as time goes
on—and that its future will involve adopting very new
forms and manifestations.

How will we assess the quality of scholarship in the future?

In Chapter 10 we discussed some of the criticisms of the
impact factor (IF), which is the currently regnant tool for
measuring quality and prestige in journal publishing.
(There is no analogous metric for monographs, which tend
to rely on positive book reviews and awards as markers of
quality and prestige.) We also touched on the emergence of
the "altmetrics" movement, which seeks to displace the IF
with tools that provide better assessment of research quality. Several of these new metrics have shown staying power
and have been adopted with varying degrees of broad
acceptance in the scholarly communication community,

while at the same time the IF shows little sign of losing its primacy as an assessment tool, whatever its weaknesses. This suggests that in the future, we will continue assessing the quality of scholarship the way we have in the past— but also in other ways. It seems likely that new tools will continue to emerge, and that they will do so in different disciplines according to the particular needs and expectations of scholars (and those who evaluate them) in those various fields.

What is the future of the research library?

This is a question that librarians have been asking themselves with increasing urgency since the advent of the World Wide Web and the subsequent migration of formal scholarly communication out of the print environment and onto an online network.

The answer depends on what one sees as the central purposes of a research library. For those who see the library primarily as a repository of carefully curated collections of physical books, journals, and other documents, the library might seem to have a dim future. As usage of physical documents in research libraries has declined and demand for more flexible and plentiful academic workspace has grown on academic campuses, books have moved out of the building—or at least out of the library's public spaces—and the amount of room given over to collaborative workspace has grown. This trend seems likely to continue.

When it comes to online documents, there are countervailing dynamics at work. On the one hand, the shift from print to online collecting has made it possible for libraries to provide more content to their patrons than ever before: Academic libraries that once subscribed to several hundred or a few thousand scholarly journals in print format now often provide access to tens of thousands of journals online. However, the massive economies of scale that the online world makes possible when it comes to information provision make it equally possible for information producers to market their wares to individual readers and researchers and offer their products at advantageous prices, thus potentially obviating the library's role as a broker of access. That role has been centrally important to the library for centuries, and to the degree that it is sidelined, existential questions arise for the library as an institution. That role has not yet disappeared, nor does it seem poised to do so in the near future, but this is an issue that does have many librarians worried. Compounding it is the fact that online access makes it easy for a library's patrons to miss the fact that the information they are accessing with such ease and speed is actually provided (often at great expense) by the library, not simply freely available online.

However, none of this means that academic and research libraries are disappearing. On many campuses, the library building is increasingly popular as a gathering spot, both for social interaction and for serious academic work. Libraries are partnering with campus programs such as academic advising, teaching-and-learning centers, and emerging digital scholarship programs, and are engaging directly in new scholarly publishing initiatives. A growing number of universities are moving their presses under the umbrella of the library organization, which has resulted in innovative new publishing programs at several major universities, notably the University of California and the University of Michigan (see Chapter 12 for further discussion of both initiatives).

Another factor that will affect the future of academic and research libraries is the trajectory of the institutions that host them. As colleges and universities change, academic libraries that are effectively aligned with them will change as well. (We will discuss some possible future changes to higher education generally in response to the next question.)

Trends seem to indicate, then, that the research library has multiple possible futures. And it also seems likely that the diversity of academic libraries will increase over time. During the print era—which, let us remember, lasted for centuries—the library of a liberal arts college looked very much like the library of a major research university, only smaller. Tomorrow, however, it may well be that different kinds of academic libraries will diverge more and more from each other both in physical design and in programming. As money gets tighter in higher education (which seems the likely future scenario both in the United States and the United Kingdom), we may well see research universities shifting their focus more and more toward science and technology fields that bring in lots of grant funding, and deemphasizing humanities and social science programs. And given the severe financial pressure that seems increasingly to be the reality for private liberal arts colleges, one has to wonder what the growth prospects are for their libraries.

What new methods of communication are evolving for scholars and scientists?

As we have discussed already in previous chapters, new communication pathways are opening up within the existing territory of scholarly journals and monographs. Open access megajournals, preprint servers, and scholarly blogs are all examples of communication channels that have come into existence just within the past couple of decades.

However, new territories are opening up as well. Social networking—as facilitated by services like LinkedIn, Mendeley, ResearchGate, and Academia.edu—has already

emerged as an important, if informal and sometimes controversial, tool for scholars who wish to share ideas and
keep up to date on professional developments. (And since
the scholarly journal evolved from scholars' and scientists'
practice of writing letters to each other, the rise of online
social networking as a locus for scholarly communication
has a rather pleasing sense of "everything old being new
again.")

ResearchGate and Academia.edu are particularly interesting examples of successful social networking services
for scholars. Both are free services that allow scholarly
authors to upload copies of their papers (in manuscript
form or as fully published pdf documents) and make them
freely available to their colleagues—or to anyone else who
happens to have signed up for the service. These services
raise potentially troubling issues as well, since they provide an easy way for authors to share papers online in
contravention of copyright laws, but they can be (and frequently are) used perfectly legally as well. Some observers
have also raised concerns about how the for-profit corporations that have set up these networks will use the data
and documents entrusted to them.[1]

Interestingly, one of the most popular social networks
for scholars and scientists is Twitter. They use it both to
perform and to archive surveys, to aggregate data, and to
crowdsource the search for secondary research sources.
Numerous applications exist that can allow researchers
to use Twitter to track trending topics both by time and
geographically, and of course tweeting is an easy way to
spread the word about one's latest project or publication.[2]

What is "digital humanism"?

The term "digital humanities" has emerged in recent years
to describe the application of computer technology and

quantitative tools to fields of scholarly inquiry associated with humanistic study rather than science or technology.

As one might imagine, there are many different ways in which digital technologies can be employed to shed new light on humanistic questions. Some of these are quite new and innovative, and others have been used for some time but are receiving new attention in light of other developments. We will discuss a few examples.

Digitization of texts and other documents

Perhaps the most fundamental (and also the most well-established) example of digital humanism is simply the process of creating and distributing digital copies of analog documents. Libraries and publishers have been doing this for years, taking rare and unique books, photographs, and other documents, creating high-quality images of them, and putting those images online. Indeed, one of the first publicly funded websites in the United States was the Library of Congress's *American Memory* project, which made high-resolution images of founding American documents like the Constitution and the Bill of Rights freely available to see and download online.[3] Since then, digitization projects have proliferated around the world and have resulted in the creation of online access to historical diaries and correspondence, government and municipal records, critical editions of historically significant books, documentary archives of important legal cases, and much more. The significance of such projects for humanistic scholarship can hardly be overstated; while it is obviously impossible to provide more than a very small number of people with actual physical access to any particular rare and unique document, it is now possible to make the intellectual content of these documents freely and easily available to billions of people at once.

Text-mining

One of the most commonly invoked examples of digital humanism is the quantitative analysis of text documents. A famous example of a text-mining tool is Google's Ngram Viewer, which allows researchers (who may be academics or simply curious members of the general public) to see the distribution over time of particular words and phrases within the millions of digitized books in the Google Books corpus.[4] Digital text-mining and analysis can also be used, for example, to inform studies of relationships between contemporaneous texts; to inform arguments about authorship; to track the development of particular word usages across regions; and to support the creation of robotic or computer-generated writing. Indeed, the ways in which digital technology might be applied to both the analysis of existing texts and the creation of new ones are limited only by the human imagination—and may not even be limited in that way if we can figure out how to use software to come up with new ideas for text-mining applications.

Geospatial studies

Geography is not only a physical science but also a human one; the study of how humans interact with the physical forms and features of their earthly environments (and how those forms and features affect human behavior) is a longstanding humanistic branch of the scientific study of the earth and its physical properties. While the study of the mutual influence of geography and human culture is not new, what has changed recently is the emergence of tools that make possible myriad new ways of studying those influences and interactions. The Alliance of Digital Humanities Organizations has formed a GeoHumanities Special Interest Group dedicated specifically to this kind of scholarship,[5] and new projects are emerging every day on campuses around the world—studying everything from the geographical distribution of published references to particular cities, to creating geographical visualizations of depositions made within different legal jurisdictions.

Critical code studies

This is a branch of digital humanism that involves the critical examination of computer code—treating code, in other words, like any other "text" that can be examined and analyzed for meaning on its own, regardless of its functional purpose as software. In other words, a particular piece of computer code may have the intended purpose of generating musical tones; however, the code itself may be said to have meanings and significance as text that tell us about the tools used to create it, about the culture and class of its creator, or about the economic circumstances of its creation—meanings and implications that, obviously, have little or nothing to do with music. This may be one of the more recondite areas of digital humanism, but it illustrates again the seemingly unbounded scope of inquiry available at the intersection of humanistic study and digital technology.

It is worth pointing out that the term "digital humanities" may itself be falling out of fashion; a preference seems to be growing for the term "digital scholarship." The latter term takes into account the fact that not all of the emerging areas of digitally powered scholarly inquiry are doing so in humanistic fields, strictly speaking; some are in areas of the social sciences in which digital technology did not until recently play a particularly important role. Nevertheless, the term "digital humanities" remains the most common one for now.

It should also be noted that digital humanism (or digital scholarship) is not without its skeptics and critics. Some look askance at the suddenly dynamic growth of digital scholarship, raising concerns of various kinds. In an influential essay in the *New Republic*, Adam Kirsh warns about the "language of scholarship" being employed in the "spirit of salesmanship" in service to "the same kind of hyperbolic, hard-sell approach we are so accustomed to hearing about the Internet, or about Apple's latest utterly revolutionary product." Indeed, he hears in the voices of digital scholarship's more enthusiastic proponents an "undertone of menace, the threat of historical illegitimacy and obsolescence. Here is the future, we are made to understand: we can either get on board or stand athwart it and get run over."[6]

Others are, if anything, even more alarmed. An essay in the *Los Angeles Review of Books* by Daniel Allington, Sarah Brouillette, and David Golumbia sees digital humanities boosterism as a neoliberal threat to academic progressivism. In their view, those who promote digital humanism see "technological innovation as an end in itself and (equate) the development of disruptive business models with political progress." The threat they see is not only ideological, however; it is also an economic problem that arises from limited resources: "The unparalleled level of material support that Digital Humanities has received," they argue, "suggests that its most significant contribution to academic politics may lie in its (perhaps unintentional) facilitation of the neoliberal takeover of the university."[7]

At this point, it seems clear both that digital humanism will continue to grow in scope and influence, and that its influence will likely continue being seen as a complicated mixture of good and bad.

NOTES

Chapter 1—Definitions and History

1. Porter, B.R. "The Scientific Journal—300th Anniversary." *Bacteriological Reviews* 1964 Sep; 28(3): 210–230.
2. https://www.aaup.org/sites/default/files/2015-16EconomicStatusReport.pdf (see especially Figure 2)
3. http://www.nature.com/news/the-future-of-the-postdoc-1.17253
4. http://www.investopedia.com/terms/b/business-ecosystem.asp

Chapter 2—Who Are the Scholars and Why Do They Communicate?

1. https://www.whitehouse.gov/sites/default/files/microsites/ostp/ostp_public_access_memo_2013.pdf
2. Cummings, W.K., & Finkelstein, M.J. "Declining Institutional Loyalty." In *Scholars in the Changing American Academy: New Contexts, New Rules, and New Roles* (pp. 131–140). Dordrecht, Heidelberg, London, New York: Springer, 2012.
3. http://classifications.carnegiefoundation.org
4. http://carnegieclassifications.iu.edu/classification_descriptions/basic.php
5. http://carnegieclassifications.iu.edu/methodology/basic.php
6. http://arxiv.org/help/general

Chapter 3—What Does the Scholarly Communication Marketplace Look Like?

1. Outsell. STM 2015 market size, share, forecast, and trend report.
2. https://www.simbainformation.com/about/release .asp?id=3880
3. Morris, S. Data about publishing. *ALPSP Alert* 2006 (112): 8.
4. https://en.wikipedia.org/wiki/List_of_university_presses
5. http://publishingperspectives.com/2011/07/ publishing-in-india-today-19000-publishers-90000-titles/
6. http://www.stm-assoc.org/2015_02_20_STM_Report_2015 .pdf
7. http://www.humanitiesindicators.org/content/indicatordoc .aspx?i=88

Chapter 4—What Is Scholarly Publishing and How Does It Work?

1. http://science.sciencemag.org/content/349/6251/aac4716
2. http://www.nature.com/news/1-500-scientists-lift-the-lid-on-reproducibility-1.19970?WT.mc_id=SFB_NNEWS_1508_RHBox
3. http://blogs.nature.com/news/2014/05/global-scientific-output-doubles-every-nine-years.html
4. https://www.ncbi.nlm.nih.gov/pmc/articles/PMC2909426/
5. http://www.slate.com/articles/health_and_science/future_tense/2016/04/biomedicine_facing_a_worse_replication_crisis_than_the_one_plaguing_psychology.html
6. http://www.infotoday.com/searcher/oct00/ tomaiuolo&packer.htm
7. http://arxiv.org
8. http://biorxiv.org
9. Several studies of academic culture have found this to be true; for some discussion of them, see Fulton, O. "Which Academic Profession Are You In?" In R. Cuthbert (ed.), *Working in Higher Education* (pp. 157–169). Buckingham: The Open University Press, 1996.
10. http://www.nature.com/nature/focus/accessdebate/22.html

Chapter 5—What Is the Role of Copyright?

1. Joyce, C., & Patterson, L.R. "Copyright in 1791: An Essay Concerning the Founders' View of Copyright Power Granted to Congress in Article 1. Section 8, Clause 8 of the U.S. Constitution." *Emory Law Journal* 2003; 52 (909). Available at SSRN: https://ssrn.com/abstract=559145

2. http://www.archives.gov/exhibits/charters/constitution_transcript.html

3. http://www.copyright.gov/circs/circ01.pdf

4. https://cyber.law.harvard.edu/property/library/moralprimer.html

5. https://www.law.cornell.edu/uscode/text/17/101

6. http://web.archive.org/web/20100109114711/; http://www.lexum.umontreal.ca/conf/dac/en/sterling/sterling.html

7. http://www.copyright.gov/title17/92chap1.html#107

8. http://www.copyright.gov/circs/circ15.pdf

9. http://www.columbia.edu/cu/provost/docs/copyright.html

10. http://www.wipo.int/treaties/en/text.jsp?file_id=283854#P68_3059

11. https://en.wikipedia.org/wiki/World_Intellectual_Property_Organization#cite_note-1

12. https://www.gnu.org/philosophy/open-source-misses-the-point.en.html

13. https://www.gnu.org/copyleft/copyleft.html

14. https://creativecommons.org/about/

15. https://en.wikipedia.org/wiki/Copyright_infringement#.22Piracy.22

16. https://en.wikipedia.org/wiki/Napster#Lawsuit

17. https://www.linkedin.com/in/elbakyan

18. http://www.mhpbooks.com/meet-the-worlds-foremost-pirate-of-academic-research/

19. http://www.nytimes.com/2016/03/13/opinion/sunday/should-all-research-papers-be-free.html?_r=0

20. https://svpow.com/2016/02/25/
does-sci-hub-phish-for-credentials/

Chapter 6—What Is the Role of the Library?

1. http://www.ingramcontent.com/publishers/print/
print-on-demand
2. http://www.lightningsource.com/ops/files/comm/
CST127/51400_CaseStudy_Oxford_NoCropmarks.pdf
3. https://www.publishing.umich.edu/projects/lever-press/
4. https://tdl.org/tdl-journal-hosting/
5. https://scoap3.org
6. http://www.projectcounter.org
7. http://www.niso.org/about/join/alliance
8. http://hathitrust.org
9. http://dp.la
10. http://www.gutenberg.org/wiki/Main_Page
11. http://memory.loc.gov
12. http://www.cdlib.org
13. http://www.digitalnc.org
14. http://digitallibrary.tulane.edu
15. https://collections.lib.utah.edu/details?id=1081984&q=%
2A&page=2&rows=25&fd=title_t%2Csetname_s%2Ctype_
t&gallery=0&facet_setname_s=uu_awm#t_1081984
16. http://lj.libraryjournal.com/2014/08/opinion/peer-to-
peer-review/asserting-rights-we-dont-have-libraries-and-
permission-to-publish-peer-to-peer-review/
17. https://www.lib.ncsu.edu/textbookservice/
18. https://www.oercommons.org

Chapter 7—The Role of University Presses

1. Meyer, S. "University Press Publishing." In P.G. Altbach & E.S.
Hoshino (eds.), *International Book Publishing: An Encyclopedia*
(pp. 354–363). New York: Garland Publishing, 1995.
2. http://global.oup.com/about/annual_report_2015/?cc=us
3. http://www.sr.ithaka.org/publications/
the-costs-of-publishing-monographs/

4. http://lj.libraryjournal.com/2011/06/academic-libraries/
   print-on-the-margins-circulation-trends-in-major-research-
   libraries/
5. http://www.aaupnet.org/images/stories/data/
   librarypresscollaboration_report_corrected.pdf
6. https://scholarlykitchen.sspnet.org/2013/07/16/having-
   relations-with-the-library-a-guide-for-university-presses/
7. https://www.insidehighered.com/news/2016/08/01/amid-
   declining-book-sales-university-presses-search-new-ways-
   measure-success
8. https://www.lib.umich.edu/news/
   michigan-publishing-collaborates-launch-lever-press

Chapter 8—Google Books and HathiTrust

1. https://books.google.com/googlebooks/about/history.html
2. http://www.nytimes.com/2015/10/29/arts/international/
   google-books-a-complex-and-controversial-experiment
   .html?_r=1
3. https://www.authorsguild.org/
   authors-guild-v-google-questions-answers/
4. http://publishers.org/news/
   publishers-sue-google-over-plans-digitize-copyrighted-books
5. http://articles.latimes.com/2009/dec/19/world/
   la-fg-france-google19-2009dec19
6. https://en.wikipedia.org/wiki/Authors_Guild,_Inc._v._
   Google,_Inc.
7. http://www.wired.com/images_blogs/threatlevel/2013/11/
   chindecision.pdf
8. https://books.google.com/ngrams
9. https://www.hathitrust.org/partnership
10. http://www.thepublicindex.org/wp-content/uploads/sites/
    19/docs/cases/hathitrust/complaint.pdf
11. https://www.library.cornell.
    edu/about/news/press-releases/
    universities-band-together-join-orphan-works-project

12. http://www.arl.org/focus-areas/court-cases/
    105-authors-guild-v-hathi-trust#.V-rdsWU34vg
13. http://www.arl.org/storage/documents/publications/
    hathitrust-decision10oct12.pdf
14. https://www.documentcloud.org/documents/1184989-12-
    4547-opn.html

Chapter 9—Needs and Practices in STM and HSS

1 https://www.researchtrends.com/issue-32-march-2013/
   trends-in-arts-humanities-funding-2004-2012/

Chapter 10—Metrics and Altmetrics

1. http://wokinfo.com/essays/impact-factor/
2. http://onlinelibrary.wiley.com/doi/10.1087/20110203/
   abstract
3. http://www.ncbi.nlm.nih.gov/pmc/articles/PMC4477767/
4. http://chronicle.com/article/the-number-thats-devouring/
   26481
5. http://www.bmj.com/content/314/7079/461.5
6. http://blogs.nature.com/news/2013/06/new-record-66-journals-
   banned-for-boosting-impact-factor-with-self-citations.html
7. https://scholarlykitchen.sspnet.org/2012/04/10/
   emergence-of-a-citation-cartel/
8. http://www.pnas.org/content/102/46/16569.full
9. http://eigenfactor.org/about.php
10. http://www.tandfonline.com/doi/abs/10.1080/
    00048623.2014.1003174?journalCode=uarl20
11. http://blogs.lse.ac.uk/impactofsocialsciences/2012/09/25/
    the-launch-of-impactstor/
12. http://plumanalytics.com
13. https://www.datacite.org/mission.html

Chapter 11—Metadata and Why It Matters

1. http://www.niso.org/publications/press/
   UnderstandingMetadata.pdf
2. http://www.metametadata.net
3. http://www.doi.org/hb.html

4. http://orcid.org/content/about-orcid

Chapter 12—Open Access: Opportunities and Challenges
1. http://www.budapestopenaccessinitiative.org/
   boai-10-recommendations
2. http://crln.acrl.org/content/76/2/88.full
3. http://poeticeconomics.blogspot.com/2012/10/cc-by-
   wrong-goal-for-open-access-and.html
4. https://www.whitehouse.gov/sites/default/files/
   microsites/ostp/ostp_public_access_memo_2013.pdf
5. https://www.martineve.com/2012/08/31/open-access-
   needs-terminology-to-distinguish-between-funding-models-
   platinum-oagold-non-apc/
6. http://www.the-scientist.com/?articles.view/articleNo/
   27376/title/Merck-published-fake-journal/
7. http://blog.historians.org/2013/07/american-historical-
   association-statement-on-policies-regarding-the-embargoing-
   of-completed-history-phd-dissertations/
8. https://scholarlykitchen.sspnet.org/2013/07/26/
   dissertation-embargoes-and-the-rights-of-scholars-aha-
   smacks-the-hornets-nest/
9. http://www.knowledgeunlatched.org
10. http://luminosoa.org
11. http://leverpress.org
12. http://caselaw.findlaw.com/us-supreme-court/499/340.html
13. https://en.wikipedia.org/wiki/Sweat_of_the_brow

**Chapter 13—Problems and Controversies in Scholarly
Communication**
1. https://www.ebscohost.com/promoMaterials/EBSCO_2017_
   Serials_Price_Projection_Report.pdf?_ga=1.114315076.2126980
   745.1477713241
2. http://www.infotoday.com/it/sep11/The-Big-Deal-Not-
   Price-But-Cost.shtml
3. https://scholarlykitchen.sspnet.org/2013/01/08/
   have-journal-prices-really-increased-in-the-digital-age/

4. See this author's comment in response to Kent Anderson's blog post cited immediately above.
5. https://scholarlykitchen.sspnet.org/2014/07/22/libraries-receive-shrinking-share/
6. http://contentz.mkt5049.com/lp/43888/438659/D187_Ebooks_Aquisition_whitepaper_v5.pdf
7. http://lj.libraryjournal.com/2011/06/academic-libraries/print-on-the-margins-circulation-trends-in-major-research-libraries/
8. http://www.dlib.org/dlib/march01/frazier/03frazier.html
9. https://web.archive.org/web/20170112125427/; https://scholarlyoa.com/
10. http://chronicle.com/article/Publisher-Threatens-to-Sue/139243/?cid=at&utm_source=at&utm_medium=en
11. https://scholarlykitchen.sspnet.org/2015/08/17/deceptive-publishing-why-we-need-a-blacklist-and-some-suggestions-on-how-to-do-it-right/

Chapter 14—The Future of Scholarly Communication
1. http://www.universityaffairs.ca/news/news-article/some-academics-remain-skeptical-of-academia-edu/
2. http://www.emeraldgrouppublishing.com/research/guides/management/twitter.htm?part=2
3. https://memory.loc.gov/ammem/index.html
4. https://books.google.com/ngrams
5. http://geohumanities.org
6. https://newrepublic.com/article/117428/limits-digital-humanities-adam-kirsch
7. https://lareviewofbooks.org/article/neoliberal-tools-archives-political-history-digital-humanities/#

INDEX

print vs. e-books, 231
readership of, 156–159, 251
reading vs. interrogating,
    158–159, 168
and royalties, 100
vs. "scholarly
    monograph," 18
vs. "trade book," 18
multimedia works, as scholarly
    products, 10

Napster, 110
National Information Standards
    Organization (NISO), 138
Ngram Viewer. *See* Google
    Ngram Viewer
NISO. *See* National
    Information Standards
    Organization (NISO)
North Carolina Digital Heritage
    Center, 139

OER. *See* open educational
    resources
open access
  and access embargoes, 205
  and article processing charge
    (APC), 205–206, 213,
    241–242
  as contested term, 198,
    202–203
  controversies surrounding,
    2–3, 209–210, 221–223
  and "copyleft"
    movement, 198

and Creative Commons, 198
  and future of scholarly
    journals, 248–249
  and HSS/STM disciplines,
    207–209
  "hybrid" publishing model,
    206–207, 248
  and libraries, 138–139
  made possible by the
    Internet, 22
  megajournals, 55–56,
    212–213, 250
  and monographs
  as online phenomenon,
    197–200
  and peer review, 65–66
  and research data sets,
    219–221
  and reuse rights, 198
  and theses and dissertations,
    213–215
  vs. "toll access," 22,
    197–202, 205
  varieties, 205–207
  vs. "public access," 203
open data. *See* open access;
    research data
open educational
    resources, 147
Open Researcher and
    Contributor ID
    (ORCID), 196
ORCID. *See* Open Researcher
    and Contributor ID
    (ORCID)